# FACTS ARE FACTS
## ORIGINAL EDITION

## BENJAMIN H. FREEDMAN

First published in 1954
Reprint edition by Last Century Media, 2023
ISBN 9781939438881

I0112023

## CONTENTS

The shoguns of the latter. Emperor Heraclius
Justinian II after his flight from Kherson to Doros.

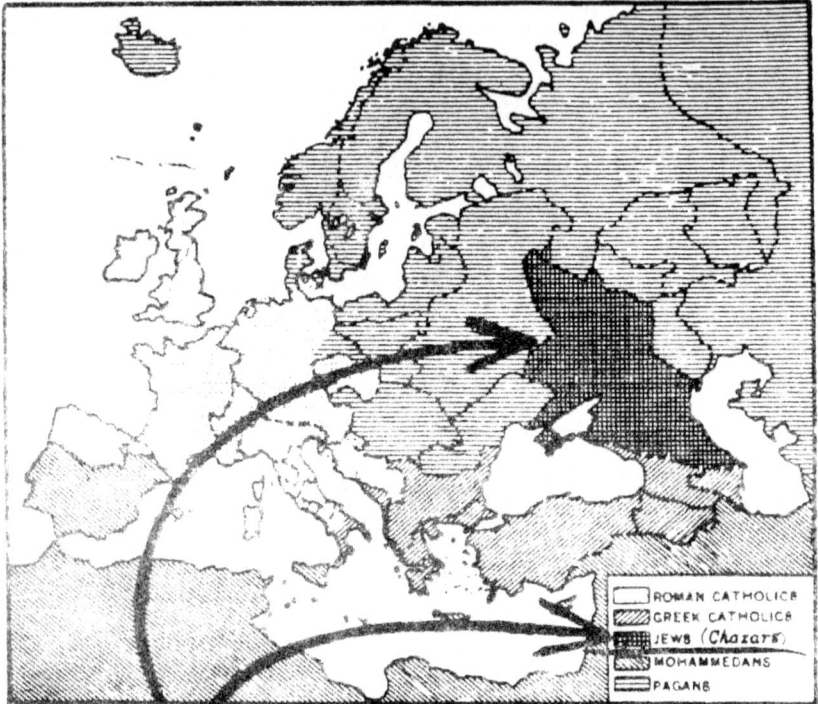

Map Showing the Distribution of Religions in Europe in the Tenth Century, C.E.,
Indicating Extent of the Kingdom of the Chazars
(After Schrader, " Atlas de Géographie Historique")

## ORIGIN OF SO-CALLED OF SELF-STYLED "JEWS" IN EASTERN EUROPE ("Khazar" is accepted modern spelling: The Jewish Encyclopedia retains the archaic "Chazar.")

The above map reveals the historic importance of so-called or self styled "Jews" in Eastern Europe in the 10th century, then still known as Khazars (Chazars) prior to the conquest of the Khazar Kingdom by the Russians in the 11th-13th centuries. The rise and fall of the Khazar Kingdom between the 1st century B.C. and the 13th century A.D. is the "key" to the solution of the world's 20th century international problems inimical to the Nations' security.

# —◦ *Dedication* ◦—

*Knowledge is a collection of facts.*

*Wisdom is the use of knowledge.*

*Without facts there is no knowledge.*

*Without knowledge there is no wisdom.*

*Facts prevent what nothing can cure.*

*Facts are Man's best defense mechanism.*

*Without them men fumble, falter and fail.*

*Without them nations decline and fall.*

*Wisdom wins wars before they start.*

*Knowledge aborts national hostilities.*

*Wisdom obviates racial antipathies.*

*Knowledge effaces religious animosities.*

*Emancipation from bigotry prefaces peace.*

*Intolerance takes all and gives nothing.*

*Peace rewards reciprocal respect and regard.*

*To all Men of Good-Will, "Pax Vobiscum!"*

— Benjamin H. Freedman

# Benjamin Freedman Speaks:
# A Jewish Defector Warns America

### by Benjamin H. Freedman

*Introductory Note:*

Benjamin H. Freedman was one of the most intriguing and amazing individuals of the 20th century. Mr. Freedman, born in 1890, was a successful Jewish businessman of New York City who was at one time the principal owner of the Woodbury Soap Company. He broke with organized Jewry after the Judeo-Communist victory of 1945, and spent the remainder of his life and the great preponderance of his considerable fortune, at least 2.5 million dollars, exposing the Jewish tyranny which has enveloped the United States. Mr. Freedman knew what he was talking about because he had been an insider at the highest levels of Jewish organizations and Jewish machinations to gain power over our nation. Mr. Freedman was personally acquainted with Bernard Baruch, Samuel Untermyer, Woodrow Wilson, Franklin Roosevelt, Joseph Kennedy, and John F. Kennedy, and many more movers and shakers of our times. This speech was given before a patriotic audience in 1961 at the Willard Hotel in Washington, D.C., on behalf of Conde McGinley's patriotic newspaper of that time, *Common Sense*. Though in some minor ways this wide-ranging and extemporaneous speech has become dated, Mr. Freedman's essential message to us — his warning to the West — is more urgent than ever before.

K.A.S.

Here in the United States, the Zionists and their co-religionists have complete control of our government. For many reasons, too many and too complex to go into here at this time, the Zionists and their co-religionists rule these United States as though they were the absolute monarchs of this country. Now you may say that is a very broad statement, but let me show you what happened while we were all asleep.

What happened? World War I broke out in the summer of 1914. There are few people here my age who remember that. Now that war was waged on one side by Great Britain, France, and Russia; and on the other side by Germany, Austria-Hungary, and Turkey.

Within two years Germany had won that war: not only won it nominally, but won it actually. The German submarines, which were a surprise to the world, had swept all the convoys from the Atlantic Ocean. Great Britain stood there without ammunition for her soldiers, with one week's food supply — and after that, starvation. At that time, the French army had mutinied. They had lost 600,000 of the flower of French youth in the defense of Verdun on the Somme. The Russian army was defecting, they were picking up their toys and going home, they didn't want to play war anymore, they didn't like the Czar. And the Italian army had collapsed.

Not a shot had been fired on German soil. Not one enemy soldier had crossed the border into Germany. And yet, Germany was offering England peace terms. They offered England a negotiated peace on what the lawyers call a status quo ante basis. That means: "Let's call the war off, and let everything be as it was before the war started." England, in the summer of 1916 was considering that — seriously. They had no choice. It was either accepting this negotiated peace that Germany was magnanimously offering them, or going on with the war and being totally defeated.

While that was going on, the Zionists in Germany, who represented the Zionists from eastern Europe, went to the British War Cabinet and — I am going to be brief because it's a long story, but I have all the documents to prove any statement that I make — they said: "Look here. You can yet win this war. You don't have to give up. You don't have to accept the negotiated peace offered to you now by Germany. You can win this war if the United States will come in as your ally." The United States was not in the war at that time. We were fresh; we were young; we were rich; we were powerful. They told England: "We will guarantee to bring the United States into the war as your ally, to fight with you on your side, if you will promise us Palestine after you win the war." In other words, they made this deal: "We will get the United States into this war as your ally. The price you must pay is Palestine after you have won the war and defeated Germany, Austria-Hungary, and Turkey." Now England had as much right to promise Palestine to anybody, as the United States would have to promise Japan to Ireland for any reason whatsoever. It's absolutely absurd that Great Britain, that never had any connection or any interest or any right in what is known as Palestine should offer it as coin of the realm to pay the Zionists for bringing the United States into the war. However, they did make that promise, in October of 1916. And shortly after that — I don't know how many here remember it — the United States, which was almost totally pro-German, entered the war as Britain's ally.

I say that the United States was almost totally pro-German because the newspapers here were controlled by Jews, the bankers were Jews, all the media of mass communications in this country were controlled by Jews; and they, the Jews, were pro-German. They were pro-German because many of them had come from Germany, and also they wanted to see Germany lick the Czar. The Jews didn't like the Czar, and they didn't want Russia to win this war. These German-Jew bankers, like Kuhn Loeb and the other big banking firms in the United States refused to finance France or England to the extent of one dollar. They stood aside and they said: "As long as France and England are tied up with Russia, not one cent!" But they poured money into Germany, they fought beside Germany against Russia, trying to lick the Czarist regime.

Now those same Jews, when they saw the possibility of getting Palestine, went to England and they made this deal. At that time, everything changed, like a traffic light that changes from red to green. Where the newspapers had been all pro-German, where they'd been telling the people of the difficulties that Germany was having fighting Great Britain commercially and in other respects, all of a sudden the Germans were no good. They were villains. They were Huns. They were shooting Red Cross nurses. They were cutting off babies' hands. They were no good. Shortly after that, Mr. Wilson declared war on Germany.

The Zionists in London had sent cables to the United States, to Justice Brandeis, saying "Go to work on President Wilson. We're getting from England what we want. Now you go to work on President Wilson and get the United States into the war." That's how the United States got into the war. We had no more interest in it; we had no more right to be in it than we have to be on the moon tonight instead of in this room. There was absolutely no reason for World War I to be our war. We were railroaded into — if I can be vulgar, we were suckered into — that war merely so that the Zionists of the world could obtain Palestine. That is something that the people of the United States have never been told. They never knew why we went into World War I.

After we got into the war, the Zionists went to Great Britain and they said: "Well, we performed our part of the agreement. Let's have something in writing that shows that you are going to keep your bargain and give us Palestine after you win the war." They didn't know whether the war would last another year or another ten years. So they started to work out a receipt. The receipt took the form of a letter, which was worded in very cryptic language so that the world at large wouldn't know what it was all about. And that was called the Balfour Declaration.

The Balfour Declaration was merely Great Britain's promise to pay the Zionists what they had agreed upon as a consideration for getting the United States into the war. So this great Balfour Declaration, that you hear so much about, is just as phony as a three dollar bill. I don't think I could make it more emphatic than that.

That is where all the trouble started. The United States got in the war. The United States crushed Germany. You know what happened. When the war ended, and the Germans went to Paris for the Paris Peace Conference in 1919 there were 117 Jews there, as a delegation representing the Jews, headed by Bernard Baruch. I was there: I ought to know. Now what happened? The Jews at that peace conference, when they were cutting up Germany and parceling out Europe to all these nations who claimed a right to a certain part of European territory, said, "How about Palestine for us?" And they produced, for the first time to the knowledge of the Germans, this

Balfour Declaration. So the Germans, for the first time realized, "Oh, so that was the game! That's why the United States came into the war." The Germans for the first time realized that they were defeated, they suffered the terrific reparations that were slapped onto them, because the Zionists wanted Palestine and were determined to get it at any cost.

That brings us to another very interesting point. When the Germans realized this, they naturally resented it. Up to that time, the Jews had never been better off in any country in the world than they had been in Germany. You had Mr. Rathenau there, who was maybe 100 times as important in industry and finance as is Bernard Baruch in this country. You had Mr. Balin, who owned the two big steamship lines, the North German Lloyd's and the Hamburg-American Lines. You had Mr. Bleichroder, who was the banker for the Hohenzollern family. You had the Warburgs in Hamburg, who were the big merchant bankers — the biggest in the world. The Jews were doing very well in Germany. No question about that. The Germans felt: "Well, that was quite a sellout."

It was a sellout that might be compared to this hypothetical situation: Suppose the United States was at war with the Soviet Union. And we were winning. And we told the Soviet Union: "Well, let's quit. We offer you peace terms. Let's forget the whole thing." And all of a sudden Red China came into the war as an ally of the Soviet Union. And throwing them into the war brought about our defeat. A crushing defeat, with reparations the likes of which man's imagination cannot encompass. Imagine, then, after that defeat, if we found out that it was the Chinese in this country, our Chinese citizens, who all the time we had thought were loyal citizens working with us, were selling us out to the Soviet Union and that it was through them that Red China was brought into the war against us. How would we feel, then, in the United States against Chinese? I don't think that one of them would dare show his face on any street. There wouldn't be enough convenient lampposts to take care of them. Imagine how we would feel.

Well, that's how the Germans felt towards these Jews. They'd been so nice to them: from 1905 on, when the first Communist revolution in Russia failed, and the Jews had to scramble out of Russia, they all went to Germany. And Germany gave them refuge. And they were treated very nicely. And here they had sold Germany down the river for no reason at all other than the fact that they wanted Palestine as a so-called "Jewish commonwealth."

Now Nahum Sokolow, and all the great leaders and great names that you read about in connection with Zionism today, in 1919, 1920, 1921, 1922, and 1923 wrote in all their papers — and the press was filled with their statements — that the feeling against the Jews in Germany is due to the fact that they realized that this great defeat was brought about by Jewish intercession in bringing the United States into the war. The Jews themselves admitted that. It wasn't that the Germans in 1919 discovered that a glass of Jewish blood tasted better than Coca-Cola or Muenschner Beer. There was no religious feeling. There was no sentiment against those people merely on account of their religious belief. It was all political. It was economic. It was anything but religious. Nobody cared in Germany whether a Jew went home and pulled down the shades and said "Shema' Yisroel" or "Our Father." Nobody cared in Germany any more than they do in the United States. Now this feeling that developed later in Germany was due to one thing: the Germans held the Jews responsible for their crushing defeat.

And World War I had been started against Germany for no reason for which Germany was responsible. They were guilty of nothing. Only of being successful. They built up a big navy. They built up world trade. You must remember that Germany at the time of the French Revolution consisted of 300 small city-states, principalities, dukedoms, and so forth. Three hundred separate little political entities. And between that time, between the times of Napoleon and Bismarck, they were consolidated into one state. And within 50 years they became one of the world's great powers. Their navy was rivaling Great Britain's, they were doing business all over the world, they could undersell anybody, they could make better products. What happened as a result of that?

There was a conspiracy between England, France, and Russia to slap down Germany. There isn't one historian in the world who can find a valid reason why those three countries decided to wipe Germany off the map politically.

When Germany realized that the Jews were responsible for her defeat, they naturally resented it. But not a hair on the head of any Jew was harmed. Not a single hair. Professor Tansill, of Georgetown University, who had access to all the secret papers of the State Department, wrote in his book, and quoted from a State Department document written by Hugo Schoenfelt, a Jew whom Cordell Hull sent to Europe in 1933 to investigate the so-called camps of political prisoners, who wrote back that he found them in very fine condition. They were in excellent shape, with everybody treated well. And they were filled with Communists. Well, a lot of them were Jews, because the Jews happened to comprise about 98 percent of the Communists in Europe at that time. And there were some priests there, and ministers, and labor leaders, and Masons, and others who had international affiliations.

Some background is in order: In 1918-1919 the Communists took over Bavaria for a few days. Rosa Luxemburg and Karl Liebknecht and a group of other Jews took over the government for three days. In fact, when the Kaiser ended the war he fled to Holland because he thought the Communists were going to take over Germany as they did Russia and that he was going to meet the same fate as the Czar. So he fled to Holland for safety, for security. After the Communist threat in Germany was quashed, the Jews were still working, trying to get back into their former status, and the Germans fought them in every way they could without hurting a single hair on anyone's head. They fought them the same way that, in this country, the Prohibitionists fought anyone who was interested in liquor. They didn't fight one another with pistols. Well, that's the way they were fighting the Jews in Germany. And at that time, mind you, there were 80 to 90 million Germans, and there were only 460,000 Jews. About one half of one percent of the population of Germany were Jews. And yet they controlled all the press, and they controlled most of the economy because they had come in with cheap money when the mark was devalued and bought up practically everything.

The Jews tried to keep a lid on this fact. They didn't want the world to really understand that they had sold out Germany, and that the Germans resented that.

The Germans took appropriate action against the Jews. They, shall I say, discriminated against them wherever they could. They shunned them. The same way that we would shun the Chinese, or the Negroes, or the Catholics, or anyone in this country who had sold us out to an enemy and brought about our defeat.

After a while, the Jews of the world called a meeting in Amsterdam. Jews from every country in the world attended this meeting in July 1933. And they said to Germany: "You fire Hitler, and you put every Jew back into his former position, whether he was a Communist or no matter what he was. You can't treat us that way. And we, the Jews of the world, are serving an ultimatum upon you." You can imagine what the Germans told them. So what did the Jews do?

In 1933, when Germany refused to surrender to the world conference of Jews in Amsterdam, the conference broke up, and Mr. Samuel Untermyer, who was the head of the American delegation and the president of the whole conference, came to the United States and went from the steamer to the studios of the Columbia Broadcasting System and made a radio broadcast throughout the United States in which he in effect said, "The Jews of the world now declare a Holy War against Germany. We are now engaged in a sacred conflict against the Germans. And we are going to starve them into surrender. We are going to use a world-wide boycott against them. That will destroy them because they are dependent upon their export business." And it is a fact that two thirds of Germany's food supply had to be imported, and it could only be imported with the proceeds of what they exported. So if Germany could not export, two thirds of Germany's population would have to starve. There was just not enough food for more than one third of the population. Now in this declaration, which I have here, and which was printed in the New York Times on August 7, 1933, Mr. Samuel Untermyer boldly stated that "this economic boycott is our means of self-defense. President Roosevelt has advocated its use in the National Recovery Administration," which some of you may remember, where everybody was to be boycotted unless he followed the rules laid down by the New Deal, and which was declared unconstitutional by the Supreme Court of that time. Nevertheless, the Jews of the world declared a boycott against Germany, and it was so effective that you couldn't find one thing in any store anywhere in the world with the words "made in Germany" on it. In fact, an executive of the Woolworth Company told me that they had to dump millions of dollars worth of crockery and dishes into the river; that their stores were boycotted if anyone came in and found a dish marked "made in Germany," they were picketed with signs saying "Hitler," "murderer," and so forth, something like these sit-ins that are taking place in the South. At a store belonging to the R. H. Macy chain, which was controlled by a family called Strauss who also happen to be Jews, a woman found stockings there which came from Chemnitz, marked "made in Germany." Well, they were cotton stockings and they may have been there 20 years, since I've been observing women's legs for many years and it's been a long time since I've seen any cotton stockings on them. I saw Macy's boycotted, with hundreds of people walking around with signs saying "murderers," "Hitlerites," and so forth. Now up to that time, not one hair on the head of any Jew had been hurt in Germany. There was no suffering, there was no starvation, there was no murder, there was nothing.

Naturally, the Germans said, "Who are these people to declare a boycott against us and throw all our people out of work, and make our industries come to a standstill? Who are they to do that to us?" They naturally resented it. Certainly they painted swastikas on stores owned by Jews. Why should a German go in and give his money to a storekeeper who was part of a boycott that was going to starve Germany into surrendering to the Jews of the world, who were going to dictate who their premier or chancellor was to be? Well, it was ridiculous.

The boycott continued for some time, but it wasn't until 1938, when a young Jew from Poland walked into the German embassy in Paris and shot a German official, that the Germans really started to get rough with the Jews in Germany. And you found them then breaking windows and having street fights and so forth.

Now I don't like to use the word "anti-Semitism" because it's meaningless, but it means something to you still, so I'll have to use it. The only reason that there was any feeling in Germany against Jews was that they were responsible for World War I and for this world-wide boycott. Ultimately they were also responsible for World War II, because after this thing got out of hand, it was absolutely necessary for the Jews and Germany to lock horns in a war to see which one was going to survive. In the meanwhile, I had lived in Germany, and I knew that the Germans had decided that Europe is going to be Christian or Communist: there is no in between. And the Germans decided they were going to keep it Christian if possible. And they started to re-arm. In November 1933 the United States recognized the Soviet Union. The Soviet Union was becoming very powerful, and Germany realized that "Our turn was going to come soon, unless we are strong." The same as we in this country are saying today, "Our turn is going to come soon, unless we are strong." Our government is spending 83 or 84 billion dollars for defense. Defense against whom? Defense against 40,000 little Jews in Moscow that took over Russia, and then, in their devious ways, took over control of many other countries of the world.

For this country now to be on the verge of a Third World War, from which we cannot emerge a victor, is something that staggers my imagination. I know that nuclear bombs are measured in terms of megatons. A megaton is a term used to describe one million tons of TNT. Our nuclear bombs had a capacity of 10 megatons, or 10 million tons of TNT, when they were first developed. Now, the nuclear bombs that are being developed have a capacity of 200 megatons, and God knows how many megatons the nuclear bombs of the Soviet Union have.

What do we face now? If we trigger a world war that may develop into a nuclear war, humanity is finished. Why might such a war take place? It will take place as the curtain goes up on Act 3: Act 1 was World War I, Act 2 was World War II, Act 3 is going to be World War III. The Jews of the world, the Zionists and their co-religionists everywhere, are determined that they are going to again use the United States to help them permanently retain Palestine as their foothold for their world government. That is just as true as I am standing here. Not alone have I read it, but many here have also read it, and it is known all over the world.

What are we going to do? The life you save may be your son's. Your boys may be on their way to that war tonight; and you don't know it any more than you knew that in 1916 in London the Zionists made a deal with the British War Cabinet to send your sons to war in Europe. Did you know it at that time? Not a person in the United States knew it. You weren't permitted to know it. Who knew it? President Wilson knew it. Colonel House knew it. Other insiders knew it.

Did I know it? I had a pretty good idea of what was going on: I was liaison to Henry Morgenthau, Sr., in the 1912 campaign when President Wilson was elected, and there was talk around the office there. I was "confidential man" to Henry Morgenthau, Sr., who was chairman of the finance committee, and I was liaison between him and Rollo Wells, the treasurer. So I sat in these meetings with President Wilson at the head of the table, and all the others, and I heard them drum into President Wilson's brain the graduated income tax and what has become the Federal Reserve, and I heard them indoctrinate him with the Zionist movement. Justice Brandeis and President Wilson were just as close as the two fingers on this hand. President Woodrow Wilson was just as incompetent when it came to determining what was going on as a newborn baby. That is how they got us into World War I, while we all slept. They sent our boys over there to be slaughtered. For what? So the Jews can have Palestine as their "commonwealth." They've fooled you so much that you don't know whether you're coming or going.

Now any judge, when he charges a jury, says, "Gentlemen, any witness who you find has told a single lie, you can disregard all his testimony." I don't know what state you come from, but in New York state that is the way a judge addresses a jury. If that witness told one lie, disregard his testimony.

What are the facts about the Jews? (I call them Jews to you, because they are known as Jews. I don't call them Jews myself. I refer to them as so-called Jews, because I know what they are.) The eastern

European Jews, who form 92 percent of the world's population of those people who call themselves Jews, were originally Khazars. They were a warlike tribe who lived deep in the heart of Asia. And they were so warlike that even the Asiatics drove them out of Asia into eastern Europe. They set up a large Khazar kingdom of 800,000 square miles. At the time, Russia did not exist, nor did many other European countries. The Khazar kingdom was the biggest country in all Europe — so big and so powerful that when the other monarchs wanted to go to war, the Khazars would lend them 40,000 soldiers. That's how big and powerful they were.

They were phallic worshippers, which is filthy and I do not want to go into the details of that now. But that was their religion, as it was also the religion of many other pagans and barbarians elsewhere in the world. The Khazar king became so disgusted with the degeneracy of his kingdom that he decided to adopt a so-called monotheistic faith — either Christianity, Islam, or what is known today as Judaism, which is really Talmudism. By spinning a top, and calling out "eeny, meeny, miney, moe," he picked out so-called Judaism. And that became the state religion. He sent down to the Talmudic schools of Pumbedita and Sura and brought up thousands of rabbis, and opened up synagogues and schools, and his people became what we call Jews. There wasn't one of them who had an ancestor who ever put a toe in the Holy Land. Not only in Old Testament history, but back to the beginning of time. Not one of them! And yet they come to the Christians and ask us to support their armed insurrections in Palestine by saying, "You want to help repatriate God's Chosen People to their Promised Land, their ancestral home, don't you? It's your Christian duty. We gave you one of our boys as your Lord and Savior. You now go to church on Sunday, and you kneel and you worship a Jew, and we're Jews." But they are pagan Khazars who were converted just the same as the Irish were converted. It is as ridiculous to call them "people of the Holy Land," as it would be to call the 54 million Chinese Moslems "Arabs." Mohammed only died in 620 A.D., and since then 54 million Chinese have accepted Islam as their religious belief. Now imagine, in China, 2,000 miles away from Arabia, from Mecca and

Mohammed's birthplace. Imagine if the 54 million Chinese decided to call themselves "Arabs." You would say they were lunatics. Anyone who believes that those 54 million Chinese are Arabs must be crazy. All they did was adopt as a religious faith a belief that had its origin in Mecca, in Arabia. The same as the Irish. When the Irish became Christians, nobody dumped them in the ocean and imported to the Holy Land a new crop of inhabitants. They hadn't become a different people. They were the same people, but they had accepted Christianity as a religious faith.

These Khazars, these pagans, these Asiatics, these Turko-Finns, were a Mongoloid race who were forced out of Asia into eastern Europe. Because their king took the Talmudic faith, they had no choice in the matter. Just the same as in Spain: If the king was Catholic, everybody had to be a Catholic. If not, you had to get out of Spain. So the Khazars became what we call today Jews. Now imagine how silly it was for the great Christian countries of the world to say, "We're going to use our power and prestige to repatriate God's Chosen People to their ancestral homeland, their Promised Land." Could there be a bigger lie than that? Because they control the newspapers, the magazines, the radio, the television, the book publishing business, and because they have the ministers in the pulpit and the politicians on the soapboxes talking the same language, it is not too surprising that you believe that lie. You'd believe black is white if you heard it often enough. You wouldn't call black black anymore — you'd start to call black white. And nobody could blame you.

That is one of the great lies of history. It is the foundation of all the misery that has befallen the world.

Do you know what Jews do on the Day of Atonement, that you think is so sacred to them? I was one of them. This is not hearsay. I'm not here to be a rabble-rouser. I'm here to give you facts. When, on the Day of Atonement, you walk into a synagogue, you stand up for the very first prayer that you recite. It is the only prayer for which you stand. You repeat three times a short prayer called the Kol Nidre. In that prayer, you enter into an agreement with God Almighty that any oath, vow, or pledge that you may make during the next twelve months shall be null and void. The oath shall not be an oath; the vow shall not be a vow; the pledge shall not be a pledge. They shall have no force or effect. And further, the Talmud teaches that whenever you take an oath, vow, or pledge, you are to remember the Kol Nidre prayer that you recited on the Day of Atonement, and you are exempted from fulfilling them. How much can you depend on their loyalty? You can depend upon their loyalty as much as the Germans depended upon it in 1916. We are going to suffer the same fate as Germany suffered, and for the same reason.

*Breaking The Silence*

960 Park Avenue
New York City

October Tenth
1954

SPECIAL DELIVERY
Dr. David Goldstein LL.D.,
Astor Post Office Station,
Boston, Massachusetts

My Dear Dr. Goldstein,

Your very outstanding achievements as a convert to Catholicism impress me as without a comparable parallel in modern history. Your devotion to the doctrine and the dogmas of the Roman Catholic Church defy any attempt at description by me only with words. Words fail me for that.

As a vigorous protagonist preserving so persistently in propagating the principles of the Roman Catholic Church, its purposes, its policies, its programs, your dauntless determination is the inspiration for countless others who courageously seek to follow in your footsteps.

In view of this fact it requires great courage for me to write to you as I am about to do. So I pray you receive this communication from me you will try to keep in mind Galatians 4:16 "Am I therefore become your enemy, because I tell you the truth?" I hope you will so favor me.

It is truly a source of great pleasure and genuine gratification to greet you at long last although of necessity by correspondence. It is quite a disappointment for me to make your acquaintance in this manner. It would now afford me a far greater pleasure and a great privilege also if instead I could greet you on this occasion in person.

Our very good mutual friend has for long been planning a meeting with you in person for me. I still wish to do that. I look forward with pleasant anticipation to doing this in the not too distant future at a time agreeable with you.

You will discover in the contents of this long letter valid evidence for the urgency on my part to communicate with you without further delay. You will further discover this urgency reflected in the present gravity of the crisis which now jeopardizes an uninterrupted continuance of the Christian faith in its long struggle as the world's most effective spiritual and social force in the Divine mission of promoting the welfare of all mankind without regard for their diversified races, religions, and nationalities.

Your most recent article coming to my attention appeared in the September issue of 'The A.P.J. Bulletin', the official publication of the organization calling themselves The Archconfraternity of Prayer for Peace and Goodwill to Israel. The headline of your article, 'News and Views of Jews', and the purpose of the organization stated in the masthead of the publication, "To Promote Interest in the Apostalate to Israel" prompts me to take Father Time by his forelock and promptly offer my comments. I beg your indulgence accordingly.

It is with reluctance that I place my comments in letter form. I hesitate to do so but I find it the only expedient thing to do under the circumstances. I beg to submit them to you now without reservations of any nature for your immediate and earnest consideration. It is my very sincere wish that you accept them in the friendly spirit in which they are submitted. It is also my hope that you will give your consideration to them and favor me with your early reply in the same friendly spirit for which I thank you in advance.

In the best interests of that worthy objective to which you are continuing to dedicate the years ahead as you have so diligently done for many past decades, I most respectfully and sincerely urge you to analyze and to study carefully the data submitted to you here. I suggest also that you then take whatever steps you consider appropriate and necessary as a result of your conclusions. In the invisible and intangible ideological war being waged in defense of the great Christian heritage against its dedicated enemies your positive attitude is vital to victory. Your passive attitude will make a negative contribution to the total effort.

You assuredly subscribe fully to that sound and sensible sentiment that "it is better to light one candle than to sit in darkness." My solitary attempts to date "to give light to them that sit in darkness, and in the shadow" may prove no more successful with you now than they have in so many other instances where I have failed during the past thirty years. In your case I feel rather optimistic at the moment.

Although not completely in vain I still live in the hope that one day on of these "candles" will burst into flame like a long smoldering spark and start a conflagration that will sweep across the nation like a prairie fire and illuminate vast new horizons for the first time. That unyielding hope is the source of the courage which aids me in my struggle against the great odds to which I am subjected for obvious reasons.

It has been correctly contended for thousands of years that "In the end Truth always prevails." We all realize that Truth in action can prove itself a dynamic power of unlimited force. But alas Truth has no self-starter. Truth cannot get off dead-center unless a worthy apostle gives Truth a little push to overcome its inertia. Without that start Truth will stand still and will never arrive at its intended destination. Truth has often died aborning for that most logical reason. Your help in this respect will prove of great value.

On the other hand Truth has many times been completely "blacked out" by repeating contradictory and conflicting untruths over and over again, and again, and again. The world's recent history supplies sober testimony of the dangers to civilization inherent in that technique. That form of treason to Truth is treachery to mankind. You must be very careful, my dear Dr. Goldstein, not to become unwittingly one of the many accessories before and after the fact who have appeared upon the scene of public affairs in recent years.

Whether unwittingly, unwillingly or unintentionally many of history's most noted characters have misrepresented the truth to the world and they have been so believed that it puzzles our generation. As recently as 1492 the world was misrepresented as flat by all the best alleged authorities on the subject. In 1492 Christopher Columbus was able to demonstrate otherwise. There are countless similar instances in the history of the world.

Whether these alleged authorities were guilty of ignorance or indifference is here beside the point. It is not important now. They were either totally ignorant of the facts or they knew the facts but chose to remain silent on the subject for reasons undisclosed by history. A duplication of this situation exists today with respect to the crisis which confronts the Christian faith. It is a vital factor today in the struggle for survival or the eventual surrender of the Christian faith to its enemies. The times in which we are living appear to be the "zero hour" for the Christian faith.

As you have observed, no institution in our modern society can long survive if its structure is not from its start erected upon a foundation of Truth. The Christian faith was first erected upon a very solid foundation of Truth by its Founder. To survive it must remain so. The deterioration, the disintegration, and finally the destruction of the structure of the Christian faith today will be accelerated in direct ratio to the extent that misrepresentation and distortion of Truth become the substitutes of Truth. Truth is an absolute quality. Truth can never be relative. There can be no degrees to Truth. Truth either exists or it does not exist. To be half-true is as incredible as to be half-honest or to be half-loyal.

As you have undoubtedly also learned, my dear Dr. Goldstein, in their attempt to do an "ounce" of good in one direction many well-intentioned persons do a "ton" of harm in another direction. We all learn that lesson sooner or later in life.

Today finds you dedicating your unceasing efforts and your untiring energy to the task of bringing so-called or self-styled "Jews" into the Roman

Catholic Church as converts. It must recall to you many times the day so many years ago when you embraced Catholicism yourself as a convert. More power to you, and the best of luck. May your efforts be rewarded with great success.

Without you becoming aware of the fact, the methods you employ contribute in no small degree to dilution of the devotion of countless Christians for their Christian faith. For each "ounce" of so-called good you accomplish by conversion of so-called or self-styled "Jews" to the Christian faith at the same time you do a "ton" of harm in another direction by diluting the devotion of countless Christians for their Christian faith. This bold conclusion on my part is asserted by me with the firm and fair conviction that the facts will support my contention. In addition it is a well-known fact that many "counterfeit" recent conversions reveal that conversions have often proved to be but "infiltrations" by latent traitors with treasonable intentions.

The attitudes you express today and your continued activity in this work require possible revision in the light of the facts submitted to you in this letter. Your present philosophy and theology on this subject seriously merit, without any delay, reconsideration on your part. What you say or write may greatly influence a "boom" or a "bust" for the Christian faith in the very near future far beyond your ability to accurately evaluate sitting in your high "white ivory tower." The Christians implicitly believe whatever you write. So do the so-called or self-styled "Jews" whom you seek to convert. This influence you wield can become a danger. I must call it to your attention.

Your reaction to the facts called to your attention in this letter can prove to be one of the most crucial verdicts ever reached bearing upon the security of the Christian faith in recent centuries. In keeping with this great responsibility I sincerely commend this sentiment to you hoping that you will earnestly study the contents of this letter from its first word to its very last word. All who know you will are in the fortunate position to know how close this subject is to your heart. By your loyalty to the high ideals you have observed during the many years you have labored so valiantly on behalf of the Christian faith you have earned the admiration you enjoy. The Christian faith you chose of your own free will in the prime of life is very proud of you in more ways than as a convert.

Regardless of what anyone anywhere and anytime in this whole wide world may say to the contrary, events of recent years everywhere establish beyond any question of a doubt that the Christian faith today stands with one foot in the grave and the other on a banana peel figuratively speaking of course. Only those think otherwise who deliberately shut their eyes to realities or who do not chose to see even with their eyes wide open. I believe you to be too realistic to indulge yourself in the futile folly of fooling yourself.

It is clear that the Christian faith today stands at the cross-roads of its destiny. The Divine and sacred mission of the Christian faith is in jeopardy today to a degree never witnessed before in its long history of almost 2000 years. The Christian faith needs loyal friends now as never before. I somehow feel that you can always be counted upon as one of its loyal friends. You cannot over-simplify the present predicament of the Christian faith. The problem it faces is too self-evident to mistake. It is in a critical situation.

When the day arrives that Christians can no longer profess their Christian faith as they profess it today in the free world the Christian faith will have seen the beginning of its "last days." What already applies to 50% of the world's total population can shortly apply equally to 100% of the world's total population. It is highly conceivable judging from present trends. The malignant character of this malady is just as progressive as cancer. It will surely prove as fatal also unless steps are taken now to reverse its course. What is now being done toward arresting its progress or reversing its trend?

My dear Dr. Goldstein, can you recall the name of the philosopher who is quoted as saying that "Nothing in this world is permanent except change?" That philosophy must be applied to the Christian faith also. The $64 question remains whether the change will be for the better or for the worse.

The problem is that simple. If the present trend continues for another 37 years in the same direction and at the same rate traveled for the past 37 years the Christian faith as it is professed today by Christians will have disappeared from the face of the earth. In what form or by what instrumentality the mission of Jesus Christ will thereupon and thereafter continue to make itself manifest here on earth is as unpredictable as it is inevitable.

In the existing crisis it is neither logical nor realistic to drive Christians out of the Christian "fold" in relatively large numbers for the dubious advantage to be obtained by bringing a comparatively small number of so-called or self-styled "Jews" into the Christian "fold".

It is useless to try to deny the fact that today finds the Christian faith on the defense throughout the world. This realization staggers the imagination of the few Christians who understand the situation. This status of the Christian faith exists in spite of the magnificent contributions of the Christian faith to the progress of humanity and civilization for almost 2000 years. It is not my intention in this letter to expose the conspirators who are dedicating themselves to the destruction of the Christian faith nor to the nature and extent of the conspiracy itself. That exposure would fill many volumes.

The history of the world for the past several centuries and current events at home and abroad confirm the existence of such a conspiracy. The world-wide network of diabolical conspirators implement this plot against the Christian faith while Christians appear to be sound asleep. The Christian clergy appear to be more ignorant or more indifferent about this conspiracy than other Christians. They seem to bury their heads in the sands of ignorance or indifference like the legendary ostrich. This ignorance or indifference on the part of the Christian clergy has dealt a blow to the Christian faith already from which it may never completely recover, if at all. It seems so sad.

Christians deserve to be blessed in this crisis with a spiritual Paul Revere to ride across the nation warning Christians that their enemies are moving in on them fast. My dear Dr. Goldstein, will you volunteer to be that Paul Revere?

Of equal importance to pin-pointing the enemies who are making war upon the Christian faith from the outside is the necessity to discover the forces at work inside the Christian faith which make it so vulnerable to its enemies on the outside. Applying yourself to this specific phase of the problem can prove of tremendous value in rendering ineffective the forces responsible for this dangerous state of affairs.

The souls of millions of Christians who are totally unknown to you are quite uneasy about the status of the Christian faith today. The minds of countless thousands among the Christian clergy are troubled by the mysterious "pressure" from above which prevents them exercising their sound judgment in this situation. If the forces being manipulated against the Christian faith from the inside can be stopped the Christian faith will be able to stand upon its feet against its enemies as the Rock of Gibraltar. Unless this can be done soon the Christian faith appears destined to crumble and to eventually collapse. An ounce of prevention is far preferable to a pound of cure you can be sure in this situation as in all others.

With all the respect due to the Christian clergy and in all humility I have an unpleasant duty to perform. I wish to go on record with you here that the Christian clergy are primarily if not solely responsible for the internal forces within the Christian faith inimical to its best interests. This conclusion on my part indicates the sum total of all the facts in my book which add up to just that. If you truly desire to be realistic and constructive you must "hew to the line and let the chips fall where they may." That is the only strategy that can save the Christian faith from a fate it does not deserve. You cannot pussy-foot with the truth any longer simply because you find that now "the truth hurts", someone you know or like.

At this late hour very little time is left in which to mend our fences if I can call it that. We are not in a position to waste any of our limited time. "Beating it around the bush" now will get us exactly nowhere. The courageous alone will endure the present crisis when all the chips are down. Figuratively and possibly literally there will be live heroes and dead cowards when the dust of this secular combat settles and not dead heroes and live cowards as sometimes occurs under other circumstances. The Christian faith today remains the only "anchor to windward" against universal barbarism. The dedicated enemies of the Christian faith have sufficiently convinced the world by this time of the savage methods they will adopt in their program to erase the Christian faith from the face of the earth.

Earlier in this letter I stated that in my humble opinion the apathy of the Christian clergy might be charged with sole responsibility for the increasing dilution of the devotion of countless Christians for the Christian faith. This is the natural consequence of the confusion created by the Christian clergy in the minds of Christians concerning certain fundamentals of the Christian faith. The guilt for this confusion rests exclusively upon Christian leadership not upon Christians generally. Confusion creates doubt. Doubt creates loss of confidence. Loss of confidence creates loss of interest. As confusion grows more, and more, and more confidence grows less, and less, and less. The result is complete loss of all interest. You can hardly disagree with that, my dear Dr. Goldstein, can you?

The confusion in the minds of Christians concerning fundamentals of the Christian faith is unwarranted and unjustified. It need not exist. It would not exist if the Christian clergy did not aid and abet the deceptions responsible for it. The Christian clergy may be shocked to learn that they have been aiding and abetting the dedicated enemies of the Christian faith. Many of the Christian clergy are actually their allies but may not know it. This phase of the current world-wide campaign of spiritual sabotage is the most negative factor in the defense of the Christian faith.

Countless Christians standing on the sidelines in this struggle see their Christian faith "withering on the vine" and about ripe enough to "drop into the lap" of its dedicated enemies. They can do nothing about it. Their cup is made more bitter for them as they observe this unwarranted and this unjustified ignorance and indifference on the part of the Christian clergy. This apathetic attitude by the Christian clergy offers no opposition to the aggressors against the Christian faith. Retreat can only bring defeat. To obviate surrender to their dedicated enemies the Christian clergy must "about face" immediately if they expect to become the victors in the invisible and intangible ideological war now being so subversively waged against the Christian faith under their very noses. When will they wake up?

If I were asked to recite in this letter the many manners in which the Christian clergy are confusing the Christian concept of the fundamentals of the Christian faith it would require volumes rather than pages to tell the whole story. Space alone compels me here to confine myself to the irreducible minimum. I will limit myself here to the most important reasons for this confusion. Brevity will of necessity limit the references cited to support the matters presented in this letter. I will do my best under the circumstances to establish the authenticity of the incontestable historical facts I call to your attention here.

In my opinion the most important reason is directly related to your present activities. Your responsibility for this confusion is not lessened by your good intentions. As you have heard said so many times "Hell is paved with good intentions." The confusion your articles create is multiplied a thousand-fold by the wide publicity given to them as a result of the very high regard in which you personally are held by editors and readers across the nation, Christian and non-Christian alike. Your articles constantly are continually reprinted and quoted from coast to coast.

The utterance by the Christian clergy which confuses Christians the most is the constantly repeated utterance that "Jesus was a Jew." That also appears to be your favorite theme. That misrepresentation and distortion of an incontestable historic fact is uttered by the Christian clergy upon the slightest pretext. They utter it constantly, also without provocation. They appear to be "trigger happy" to utter it. They never miss an opportunity to do so. Informed intelligent Christians cannot reconcile this truly unwarranted misrepresentation and distortion of an incontestable historic fact by the Christian clergy with information known by them now to the contrary which comes to them from sources believed by them to be equally reliable.

This poses a serious problem today for the Christian clergy. They can extricate themselves from their present predicament now only be resorting to "the truth, the whole truth, and nothing but the truth". That is the only formula by which the Christian clergy can recapture the lost confidence of Christians. As effective spiritual leaders they cannot function without this lost confidence. They should make that their first order of business.

My dear Dr. Goldstein, you are a theologian of high rank and a historian of note. Of necessity you also should agree with other outstanding authorities on the subject of whether "Jesus was a Jew." These leading authorities agree today that there  is no foundation in fact for the implications, inferences and the innuendoes resulting from the incorrect belief that "Jesus was a Jew". Incontestable historic facts and an abundance of other proofs establish beyond the possibility of any doubt the incredibility of the assertion so often heard today that "Jesus was a Jew".

Without any fear of contradiction based upon fact the most competent and best qualified authorities all agree today that Jesus Christ was not a so-called or self-styled "Jew". They do confirm that during His lifetime Jesus was known as a "Judean" by His contemporaries and not as a "Jew", and that Jesus referred to

Himself as a "Judean" and not as a "Jew".

During His lifetime here on earth Jesus was referred to by contemporary historians as a "Judean" and not as a "Jew." Contemporary theologians of Jesus whose competence to pass upon this subject cannot challenge by anyone today also referred to Jesus during his lifetime here on earth as a "Judean" and not as a "Jew".

Inscribed upon the Cross when Jesus was crucified were the Latin words "Jesus Nazarenus Rex Iudeorum". Pontius Pilate's mother-tongue. No one will question the fact that Pontius Pilate was well able to accurately express his own ideas in his own mother-tongue. The authorities competent to pass upon the correct translation into English of the Latin "Jesus Nazarenus Rex Iudeorum" agree that it is "Jesus of Nazarene Ruler of the Judeans." There is no disagreement upon that by them.

During His lifetime here on earth Jesus was not regarded by Pontius Pilate nor by the Judeans among whom He dwelt as "King of the Jews". The inscription on the Cross upon which Jesus was crucified has been incorrectly translated into the English language only since the 18th century. Pontius Pilate was ironic and sarcastic when he ordered inscribed upon the cross the Latin words "Jesus Nazarenus Rex Iudeorum".

About to be crucified, with the approval of Pontius Pilate, Jesus was being mocked by Pontius Pilate. Pontius Pilate was well aware at that time that Jesus had been denounced, defied and denied by the Judeans who alas finally brought about His Crucifixion as related by history.

Except for His few followers at that time in Judea all other Judeans abhorred Jesus and detested His teachings and the things for which He stood. That deplorable fact cannot be erased from history by time. Pontius Pilate was himself the "ruler" of the Judeans at the time he ordered inscribed upon the cross in Latin words "Jesus Nazarenus Rex Iudeorum", In English "Jesus the Nazarene Ruler of the Judeans". But Pontius Pilate never referred to himself as "ruler" of the Judeans. The ironic and sarcastic reference of Pontius Pilate to Jesus as "Ruler of the Judeans" can hardly be accepted as recognition by Pontius Pilate of Jesus as "Ruler of the Judeans". That is inconceivable by any interpretation.

At the time of the Crucifixion of Jesus Pontius Pilate was the administrator in Judea for the Roman Empire. At that time in history the area of the Roman Empire included a part of the Middle East. As far as he was concerned officially or personally the inhabitants of Judea were "Judeans" to Pontius Pilate and not so-called "Jews" as they have been styled since the 18th century. In the time of Pontius Pilate and not so-called "Jews" as they have been styled since the 18th century. In the time of Pontius Pilate in history there was no religious, racial or national group in Judea known as "Jews" nor had there been any group so identified anywhere else in the world prior to that time.

Pontius Pilate expressed little interest as the administrator of the Roman Empire officially or personally in the wide variety of forms of religious worship then practiced in Judea. These forms of religious worship extended from phallic worship and other forms of idolatry to the emerging spiritual philosophy of an eternal, omnipotent and invisible divine deity, the emerging Yahve (Jehovah) concept which predated Abraham of Bible fame by approximately 2000 years. As the administrator for the Roman Empire in Judea it was the official policy of Pontius Pilate never to interfere in the spiritual affairs of the local population. Pontius Pilate's primary responsibility was the collection of taxes to be forwarded home to Rome, not the forms of religious worship practiced by the Judeans from whom those taxes were collected.

As you well know, my dear Dr. Goldstein, the Latin word "rex" means "ruler, leader" in English. During the lifetime of Jesus in Judea the Latin word "rex" meant only that to Judeans familiar with the Latin language. The Latin word "rex" is the Latin verb "rego, regere, rexi, rectus" in English means as you also well know "to rule, to lead". Latin was of course the official language in all the provinces administered by a local administrator of the Roman Empire. This fact accounts for the inscription on the cross in Latin.

With the invasion of the British Isles by the Anglo-Saxons, the English language substituted the Anglo-Saxon "king" for the Latin equivalent "rex" used before the Anglo-Saxon invasion. The adoption of "king" for "rex" at this late date in British history did not retroactively alter the meaning of the Latin "rex" to the Judeans in the time of Jesus. The Latin "rex" to them then meant only "ruler, leader" as it still means in Latin. Anglo-Saxon "king" was spelled differently when first used but at all times meant the same as "rex" in Latin, "leader" of a tribe.

During the lifetime of Jesus it was very apparent to Pontius Pilate that Jesus was the very last Person in Judea the Judeans would select as their "ruler" or their "leader". In spite of this situation in Judea Pontius Pilate did not hesitate to order the inscription of the cross "Jesus Nazarenus Rex Iudeorum". By the wildest stretch of the imagination it is not conceivable that this sarcasm and irony by Pontius Pilate at the time of the crucifixion was not solely mockery of Jesus by Pontius Pilate and only mockery. After this reference to "Jesus the Nazarene Ruler of the Judeans" the Judeans forthwith proceeded to crucify Jesus upon that very cross.

In Latin in the lifetime of Jesus the name of the political subdivision in the Middle East known in modern history as Palestine was "Iudaea". It was then administered by Pontius Pilate as administrator for the Roman Empire of which it was then a part. The English for the Latin "Iudaea" is "Judea".

English "Judean" is the adjective for the noun "Judea". The ancient native population of the subdivision in the Middle East known in modern history as Palestine was then called "Iudaeus" in Latin and "Judean" in English. Those words identified the indigenous population of Judea in the lifetime of Jesus. Who can deny that Jesus was a member of the indigenous population of Judea in His lifetime?

And of course you know, my dear Dr. Goldstein, in Latin the Genitive Plural of "Iudaeus" is "Iudaeorum". The English translation of the Genitive Plural of "Iudaeorum" is "of the Judeans". It is utterly impossible to give any other English translation to "Iudaeorum" than "of the Judeans". Qualified and competent theologians and historians regard as incredible any other translation into English of "Jesus Nazarenus Rex Iudaeorum" than "Jesus the Nazarene Ruler of the Judeans". You must agree that this is literally correct.

At the time Pontius Pilate was ordering the "Jesus Nazarenus Rex Iudaeorum" inscribed upon the Cross the spiritual leaders of Judea were protesting to Pontius Pilate "not to write that Jesus was the ruler of the Judeans" but to inscribe instead that Jesus "had said that He was the ruler of the Judeans". The spiritual leaders of Judea made very strong protests to Pontius Pilate against his reference to Jesus as "Rex Iudaeorum" insisting that Pontius Pilate was not familiar with or misunderstood the status of Jesus in Judea. These protests are a matter of historical record, as you know.

The spiritual leaders in Judea protested in vain with Pontius Pilate. They insisted that Jesus "had said that He was the ruler of the Judeans" but that Pontius Pilate was "not to write that Jesus was the ruler of the Judeans". For after all Pontius Pilate was a foreigner in Judea who could not understand the local situations as well as the spiritual leaders. The intricate pattern of the domestic political, social and economic cross-currents in Judea interested Pontius Pilate very little as Rome's administrator.

The Gospel by John was written originally in the Greek language according to the best authorities. In the Greek original there is no equivalent for the English that Jesus "had said that He was the ruler of the Judeans". The English translation of the Greek original of the Gospel by John, XIX, 19, reads "Do not inscribe 'the monarch (basileus) of the Judeans (Ioudaios), but that He Himself said I am monarch (basileus) of the Judeans (Ioudaios)' ". "Ioudaia" is the Greek for the Latin for "basileus" in Greek. The English "ruler", or its alternative "leader", define the sense of Latin "rex" and Greek "basileus" as they were used in the Greek and Latin Gospel of John.

Pontius Pilate "washed his hands" of the protests by the spiritual leaders in Judea who demanded of him that the inscription on the cross authored by

Pontius Pilate be corrected in the manner they insisted upon. Pontius Pilate be corrected in the manner they insisted upon. Pontius Pilate very impatiently replied to their demands "What I have written, I have written." The inscription on the cross remained what it had been, "Jesus Nazarenus Rex Iudaeorum", or "Jesus the Nazarene Ruler of the Judeans" in English.

The Latin quotations and words mentioned in this letter are verbatim quotations and the exact words which appear in the 4th century translation of the New Testament into Latin by St. Jerome. This translation is referred to as the Vulgate Edition of the New Testament. It was the first official translation of the New Testament into Latin made by the Christian Church. Since that time it has remained the official New Testament version used by the Catholic Church. The translation of the Gospel of John into Latin by St. Jerome was made from the Greek language in which the Gospel of John was originally written according to the best authorities on this subject.

The English translation of the gospel by John XIX, 19, from the original text in the Greek language reads as follows, "Pilate wrote a sign and fastened it to the Cross and the writing was "Jesus the Nazarene the monarch of the Judeans' ". In the original Greek manuscript there is mention also made of the demands upon Pontius Pilate by the spiritual leaders in Judea that Pontius Pilate alter the reference on the cross to Jesus as "Ruler of the Judeans". The Greek text of the original manuscript of the Gospel by John establishes beyond any question or doubt that the spiritual leaders in Judea at that time had protested to Pontius Pilate that Jesus was "not the ruler of the Judeans" but only "had said that He was the ruler of the Judeans".

There is no factual foundation in history or theology today for the implications, inferences and innuendoes that the Greek "Ioudaios", the Latin "Iudaeus", or the English "Judean:" ever possessed a valid religious connotation. In their three respective languages these three words have only indicated a strictly topographical or geographical connotation. In their correct sense these three words in their respective languages were used to identify the members of the indigenous native population of the geographic area known as Judea in the lifetime of Jesus. During the lifetime of Jesus there was not a form of religious worship practiced in Judea or elsewhere in the known world which bore a name even remotely resembling the name of the political subdivision of the Roman Empire; i.e., "Judaism" from "Judea". No cult or sect existed by such a name.

It is an incontestable fact that the word "Jew" did not come into existence until the year 1775. Prior to 1775 the word "Jew" did not exist in any language. The word "Jew" was introduced into the English for the first time in the 18th century when Sheridan used it in his play "The Rivals", II, i, "She shall have a skin like a mummy, and the beard of a Jew". Prior to this use of the word "Jew" in the English language by Sheridan in 1775 the word "Jew" had not become a word in the English language. Shakespeare never saw the word "Jew" as you will see. Shakespeare never used the word "Jew" in any of his works, the common general belief to the contrary notwithstanding. In his "Merchant of Venice", V.III.i.61, Shakespeare wrote as follows: "what is the reason? I am a Iewe; hath not a Iewe eyes?".

In the Latin St. Jerome 4th century Vulgate Edition of the New Testament Jesus is referred to by the Genitive Plural of "Iudaeus" in the Gospel of John reference to the inscription on the Cross, - "Iudaeorum". It was in the 4th century that St. Jerome translated into Latin the manuscripts of the New Testament from the original languages in which they were written. This translation by St. Jerome is referred to still today as the Vulgate Edition by the Roman Catholic Church authorities, who use it today.

Jesus is referred as a so-called "Jew" for the first time in the New Testament in the 18th century. Jesus is first referred to as a so-called "Jew" in the revised 18th century editions in the English language of the 14th century first translations of the New Testament into English. The history of the origin of the word "Jew" in the English language leaves no doubt that the 18th century "Jew" is the 18th century contracted and corrupted English word for the 4th century Latin "Iudaeus" found in St. Jerome's Vulgate Edition. Of that there is no longer doubt.

The available manuscripts from the 4th century to the 18th century accurately trace the origin and give the complete history of the word "Jew" in the English language. In these manuscripts are to be found all the many earlier English equivalents extending through the 14 centuries from the 4th to the 18th century. From the Latin "Iudaeus" to the English "Jew" these English forms included successively: "Gyu", "Giu", "Iu", "Iuu", "Iuw", "Ieuu", "Ieuy", "Iwe", "Iow", "Iewe", "Ieue", "Iue", "Ive", "Iew", and then finally in the 18th century, "Jew". The many earlier English equivalents for "Jews" through the 14 centuries are "Giwis", "Giws", "Gyues", "Gywes", "Giwes", "Geus", "Iuys", "Iows", "Iouis", "Iews", and then also finally in the 18th century, "Jews".

With the rapidly expanding use in England in the 18th century for the first time in history of the greatly improved printing presses unlimited quantities of the New Testament were printed. These revised 18th century editions of the earlier 14th century first translations into the English language were then widely distributed throughout England and the English speaking world among families who had never possessed a copy of the New Testament in any language. In these 18th century editions with revisions the word "Jew" appeared for the first time in any English translations. The word "Jew" as it was used in the 18th century editions has since continued in use in all elections of the New Testament in the English language. The use of the word "Jew" thus was stabilized.

As you know, my dear Dr. Goldstein, the best known 18th century editions of the New Testament in English are the Rheims (Douai) Edition and the King James Authorized Edition. The Rheims (Douai) translation of the New Testament into English was first printed in 1582 but the word "Jew" did not appear in it. The King James Authorized translation of the New Testament into English was begun in 1604 and first published in 1611. The word "Jew" did not appear in it either. The word "Jew" appeared in both these well-known editions in their 18th century revised versions for the first times.

Countless copies of the revised 18th century editions of the Rheims (Douai) and the King James translations of the New Testament into English were distributed to the clergy and the laity throughout the English speaking world. They did not know the history of the origin of the English word "Jew" nor did they care. They accepted the English word "Jew" as the only and as the accepted form of the Latin "Iudaeus" and the Greek "Ioudaios". How could they be expected to have known otherwise? The answer is they could not and they did not. It was a new English word to them.

When you studied Latin in your school days you were taught that the letter "I" in Latin when used as the first letter in a word is pronounced like the letter "Y" in English when it is the first letter in words like "yes", "youth" and "yacht". The "I" in "Iudaeus" is pronounced like the "Y" in "yes", "youth", and "yacht" in English. In all the 4th century to 18th century forms for the 18th century "Jew" the letter "I" was pronounced like the English "Y" in "yes", "youth", and "yacht". The same is true of the "Gi" or the "Gy" where it was used in place of the letter "I".

The present pronunciation of the word "Jew" in modern English is a development of recent times. In the English language today the "J" in "Jew" is pronounced like the "J" in the English "justice", "jolly", and "jump". This is the case only since the 18th century. Prior to the 18th century the "J" in "Jew" was pronounced exactly like the "Y" in the English "yes", "youth", and "yacht". Until the 18th century and perhaps even later than the 18th century the word "Jew" in English was pronounced like the English "you" or "hew", and the word "Jews" like "youse" or "hews". The present pronunciation of "Jew" in English is a new pronunciation acquired after the 18th century.

The German language still retains the Latin original pronunciation. The German "Jude" is the German equivalent of the English "Jew". The "J" in the German "Jude" is pronounced exactly like the English "Y" in "yes", "youth", and "yacht". The German "J" is the equivalent of the Latin "I" and both are pronounced exactly like the English "Y" in "yes", "youth" and "yacht". The German "Jude" is virtually the first syllable of the Latin "Iudaeus" and is pronounced exactly like it. The German "Jude" is the German contraction and corruption of the Latin "Iudaeus" just as the English "Jew" is the contraction and corruption of the Latin "Iudaeus". The German "J" is always pronounced like the English "Y" in "yes", "youth", and "yacht" when it is the first letter of a word. The pronunciation of the "J" in German "Jude" is not an exception to the pronunciation of the "J" in German.

The English language as you already know, my dear Dr. Goldstein, is largely made up of words adopted from foreign languages. After their adoption by the English language foreign words were then adapted by contracting their spelling and corrupting their foreign pronunciation to make them more easily pronounced in English from their English spelling. This process of first adopting foreign words and then adapting them by contracting their spelling and corrupting their pronunciation resulted in such new words in the English language as "cab" from the French "cabriolet" and many thousands of other words similarly from their original foreign spelling. Hundreds of others must come to your mind.

By this adopting-adapting process the Latin "Iudacus" and the Greek "Ioudaios" finally emerged in the 18th century as "Jew" in the English language. The English speaking peoples struggled through 14 centuries seeking to create for the English language an English equivalent for the Latin "Iudaeus" and the Greek "Ioudaios" which could be easily pronounced in English from its English spelling. The English "Jew" was the resulting 18th century contracted and corrupted form of the Latin "Iudaeus" and the Greek "Ioudaios". The English "Jew" is easily pronounced in English from its English spelling. The Latin "Iudaeus" and the Greek "Ioudaios" cannot be as easily pronounced in English from the Latin and Greek spelling. They were forced to coin a word.


The earliest version of the New Testament in English from the Latin Vulgate Edition is the Wyclif, or Wickliffe Edition published in 1380. In the Wyclif Edition Jesus is there mentioned as One of the "iewes". That was the 14th century English version of the Latin "Iudaeus" and was pronounced "hew-weeze", in the plural, and "iewe" pronounced "hew-wee" in the singular. In the 1380 Wyclif Edition in English the Gospel by John, XIX.19, reads "Ihesus of nazareth kyng of the iewes". Prior to the 14th century the English language adopted the Anglo-Saxon "kyng" together with many other Anglo-Saxon words in place of the Latin "rex" and the Greek "basileus". The Anglo-Saxon also meant "tribal leader".

In the Tyndale Edition of the New Testament in English published in 1525

Jesus was likewise described as One of the "Iewes". In the Coverdale Edition published in 1535 Jesus was also described as One of the "Iewes". In the Coverdale Edition the Gospel by John, XIX.19, reads "Iesus the Nazareth, kynge of the "Iewes". In the Cranmer Edition published in 1539 Jesus was again described as One of the "Iewes". In the Geneva Edition published in 1540-1557 Jesus was also described as One of the "Iewes". In the Rheims Edition published in 1582 Jesus was described as One of the "Ievves". In the King James Edition published in 1604-1611 also known as the Authorized Version Jesus was described again as one of the "Iewes". The forms of the Latin "Iudaeus" were used which were current at the time these translations were made.

The translation into English of the Gospel by John, XIX.19, from the Greek in which it was originally written reads "Do not inscribe `the monarch of the Judeans' but that He Himself said `I am monarch' ". In the original Greek manuscript the Greek "basileus" appears for "monarch" in the English and the Greek "Ioudaios" appears for "Judeans" in the English. "Ioudaia" in Greek is "Judea" in English. "Ioudaios" in Greek is "Judeans" in English. There is no reason for any confusion.

My dear Dr. Goldstein, if the generally accepted understanding today of the English "Jew" and "Judean" conveyed the identical implications, inferences and innuendoes as both rightly should, it would make no difference which of these two words was used when referring to Jesus in the New Testament or elsewhere. But the implications, inferences, and innuendoes today conveyed by these two words are as different as black is from white. The word "Jew" today is never regarded as a synonym for "Judean" nor is "Judean" regarded as a synonym for "Jew".

As I have explained, when the word "Jew" was first introduced into the English language in the 18th century its one and only implication, inference and innuendo was "Judean". However during the 18th, 19th and 20th centuries a well-organized and well- financed international "pressure group" created a so-called "secondary meaning" for the word "Jew" among the English-speaking peoples of the world. This so-called "secondary meaning" for the word "Jew" bears no relation whatsoever to the 18th century original connotation of the word "Jew". It is a misrepresentation.

The "secondary meaning" of the word "Jew" today bears as little relation to its original and correct meaning as the "secondary meaning" today as for the word "camel" bears to the original and correct meaning of the word "camel", or the "secondary meaning" for the word "ivory" bears to the original and correct meaning of the word "ivory". The "secondary meaning" today for the word "camel" is a  cigarette by that name but its original and correct meaning is a desert animal by that ancient name. The "secondary meaning" of the word "ivory" today is a piece of soap but its original and correct meaning is the tusk of a male elephant.

The "secondary meaning" of words often become the generally accepted meanings of words formerly having entirely different meanings. This is accomplished by the expenditure of great amounts of money for well-planned publicity. Today if you ask for a "camel" someone will hand you a cigarette by that name. Today if you ask for a piece of "ivory" someone will hand you a piece of soap by that name. You will never receive either a desert animal or a piece of the tusk of a male elephant. That must illustrate the extent to which these "secondary meanings" are able to practically eclipse the original and correct meanings of words in the minds of the general public. The "secondary meaning" for the word "Jew" today has practically totally eclipsed the original and correct meaning of the word "Jew" when it was introduced as a word in the English language. This phenomena is not uncommon.

The United States Supreme Court has recognized the "secondary meaning" of words. The highest court in the land has established as basic law that "secondary meanings" can acquire priority rights to the use of any dictionary word.

Well-planned and well-financed world-wide publicity through every available media by well-organized groups of so-called or self-styled "Jews" for three centuries has created a "secondary meaning" for the word "Jew" which has completely "blacked out" the original and correct meaning of the word "Jew".

There can be no doubt about that.

There is not a person in the whole English-speaking world today who regards a "Jew" as a "Judean" in the literal sense of the word. That was the correct and only meaning in the 18th century. The generally accepted "secondary meaning" of the word "Jew" today with practically no exceptions is made up of four almost universally-believed theories. These four theories are that a so-called or self-styled "Jew" is (1) a person who today professes the form of religious worship known as "Judaism", (2) a person who claims to belong to a racial group associated with the ancient Semites, (3) a person directly the descendant of an ancient nation which thrived in Palestine in Bible history, (4) a person blessed by Divine intentional design with certain superior cultural characteristics denied to other racial, religious or national groups, all rolled into one.

The present generally accepted "secondary meaning" of the word "Jew" is fundamentally responsible for the confusion in the minds of Christians regarding elementary tenets of the Christian faith. It is likewise responsible today to a very great extent for the dilution of the devotion of countless

Christians for their Christian faith. The implications, inferences and innuendoes of the word "Jew" today, to the preponderant majority of intelligent and informed Christians, is contradictory and in complete conflict with incontestable historic fact. Christians who cannot be fooled any longer are suspect of the Christian clergy who continue to repeat, and repeat, and repeat ad nauseam their pet theme song "Jesus was a Jew". It actually now approaches a psychosis.

Countless Christians know today that they were "brain washed" by the Christian clergy on the subject "Jesus was a Jew". The resentment they feel is not yet apparent to the Christian clergy. Christians now are demanding from the Christian clergy, "the truth, the whole truth, and nothing but the truth". It is now time for the Christian clergy to tell Christians what they should have told them long ago. Of all religious groups in the world Christians appear to be the least informed of any on the subject. Have their spiritual leaders been reckless with the truth?

Countless intelligent and informed Christians no longer accept unchallenged assertions by the Christian clergy that Jesus in His lifetime was a member of a group in Judea which practiced a religious form of worship then which is today called "Judaism", or that Jesus in His lifetime here on earth was a member of the racial group which today includes the preponderant majority of all so-called or self-styled "Jews" in the world, or that the so-called or self-styled "Jews" throughout the world today are the lineal descendants of the nation in Judea of which Jesus was a national in His lifetime here on earth, or that the cultural characteristics of so-called or self-styled "Jews" throughout the world today correspond with the cultural characteristics of Jesus during His lifetime here on earth and His teachings while He was here on earth for a brief stay. Christians will no longer believe that the race, religion, nationality and culture of Jesus and the race, religion, nationality and culture of so-called or self-styled "Jews" today or their ancestors have a common origin or character.

The resentment by Christians is more ominous than the Christian clergy suspect. Under existing conditions the Christian clergy will find that ignorance is not bliss, nor wisdom folly. Christians everywhere today are seeking to learn the authentic relationship between the so-called or self-styled "Jews" through-out the world today and the "Judeans" who populated "Judea" before, during and after the time of Jesus. Christians now insist that they be told correctly by the Christian clergy about the racial, religious, national and cultural background of the so-called or self-styled "Jews" throughout the world today and the basis for associating these backgrounds with the racial, religious, national and cultural background of Jesus in His lifetime in Judea. The intelligent and informed Christian are alerted to the exploded myth that the so-called or self-styled "Jews" throughout the world today are the direct descendants of the "Judeans" amongst whom Jesus lived during His lifetime here on earth.

Christians today are also becoming more and more alerted day by day why the so-called or self-styled "Jews" throughout the world for three centuries have spent uncounted sums of money to manufacture the fiction that the "Judeans" in the time of Jesus were "Jews" rather than "Judeans", and that "Jesus was a Jew". Christians are becoming more and more aware day by day of all the economic and political advantages accruing to the so-called or self-styled "Jews" as a direct result of their success in making Christians believe that "Jesus was a Jew" in the "secondary meaning" they have created for the 18th century word "Jew". The so-called or self-styled "Jews" throughout the world today represent themselves to Christians as "Jews" only in the "secondary meaning" of the word "Jew". They seek to thereby prove their kinship with Jesus. They emphasize this fiction to Christians constantly. That fable is fast fading and losing its former grip upon the imaginations of Christians.

To allege that "Jesus was a Jew" in the sense that during His lifetime Jesus professed and practiced the form of religious worship known and practiced under the modern name of "Judaism" is false and fiction of the most blasphemous nature. If to be a so-called or self-styled "Jew" then or now the practice of "Judaism" was a requirement then Jesus certainly was not a so-called "Jew". Jesus abhorred and denounced the form of religious worship practiced in Judea in His lifetime and which is known and practiced today under its new name "Judaism". That religious belief was then known as "Pharisiasm". The Christian clergy learned that in their theological seminary days but they have never made any attempt to make that clear to Christians.

The eminent Rabbi Louis Finkelstein, the head of The Jewish Theological Seminary of America, often referred to as "The Vatican of Judaism", in his Foreword to his First Edition of his world-famous classic "The Pharisees, The Sociological Background of Their Faith", on page XXI states:

"...Judaism...Pharisiasm became Talmudism, Talmudism became Medieval Rabbinism, and Medieval Rabbinism became Modern Rabbinism. But throughout these changes in name...the spirit of the ancient Pharisees survives, unaltered...From Palestine to Babylonia; from Babylonia to North Africa, Italy, Spain, France and Germany; from these to Poland, Russia, and eastern Europe generally, ancientharisaism has wandered...demonstrates the enduring importance which attaches to Pharisaism as a religious movement..."

The celebrated Rabbi Louis Finkelstein in his great classic quoted from above traces the origin of the form of religious worship practiced today under the present name "Judaism", to its origin as "Pharisaism" in Judea in the time of Jesus.

Rabbi Louis Finkelstein confirms what the eminent Rabbi Adolph Moses states in his great classic "Yahvism, and Other Discourses", in collaboration with the celebrated Rabbi H.G. Enlow, published in 1903 by the Louisville Section of the Council of Jewish Women, in which Rabbi Adolph Moses, on page 1, states:

"Among the innumerable misfortunes which have befallen...the most fatal in its consequences is the name Judaism...Worse still, the Jews themselves, who have gradually come to call their religion Judaism...Yet, neither in biblical nor post-biblical, neither in talmudic, nor in much later times, is the term Judaism ever heard...the Bible speaks of the religion...as "Torah Yahve", the instruction, or the moral law revealed by Yahve...in other places...as "Yirath Yahve", the fear and reverence of Yahve.

These and other appellations CONTINUED FOR MANY AGES TO STAND FOR THE RELIGION...To distinguish it from Christianity and Islam, the Jewish philosophers sometimes designate it as the faith or belief of the Jews ... IT WAS FLAVIUS JOSEPHUS, WRITING FOR THE INSTRUCTION OF GREEKS AND ROMANS, WHO COINED THE TERM JUDAISM, in order to pit it against Hellenism...by Hellenism was understood the civilization, comprising language, poetry, religion, art, science, manners, customs, institutions, which...had spread from Greece, its original home, over vast regions of Europe, Asia and Africa...The Christians eagerly seized upon the name...the Jews themselves, who intensely detested the traitor Josephus, refrained from reading his works...HENCE THE TERM JUDAISM COINED BY JOSEPHUS REMAINED ABSOLUTELY UN-KNOWN TO THEM...IT WAS ONLY IN COMPARATIVELY RECENT TIMES, AFTER THE JEWS BECAME FAMILIAR WITH MODERN CHRISTIAN LITERATURE, THAT THEY BEGAN TO NAME THEIR RELIGION JUDAISM." (emphasis supplied).

This statement by the world's two leading authorities on this subject clearly establishes beyond any question or any doubt that so-called "Judaism" was not the name of any form of religious worship practiced in Judea in the time of Jesus. The Flavius Josephus referred to in the above quotation lived in the 1st century. It was he who coined the word "Judaism" in the 1st century explicitly for the purpose recited clearly above. Religious worship known and practiced today under the name of "Judaism" by so-called or self-styled "Jews" throughout the world was known and practiced in Judea in the time of Jesus under the name "Pharisaism" according to Rabbi Louis Finkelstein, head of the Jewish Theological Seminary of America, and all the other most competent and qualified recognized authorities on the subject.

The form of religious worship known as "Pharisaism" in Judea in the time of Jesus was a religious practice based exclusively upon the Talmud. The

Talmud in the time of Jesus was the Magna Charta, the Declaration of Independence, the Constitution, and the Bill of Rights, ALL ROLLED INTO ONE, of those who practiced "Pharisaism". The Talmud today occupies the same relative position with respect to those who profess "Judaism". The Talmud today virtually exercises totalitarian dictatorship over the lives of so-called or self-styled "Jews" whether they are aware of that fact or not. Their spiritual leaders make no attempt to conceal the control they exercise over the lives of so-called or self-styled "Jews".

They extend their authority far beyond the legitimate limits of spiritual matters. Their authority has no equal outside religion.

The role of the Talmud plays in "Judaism" as it is practiced today is officially stated by the eminent Rabbi Morris N. Kertzer, the Director of Inter-religious Activities of the North American Jewish Committee and the President of the Jewish Chaplains Association of the Armed Forces of the United States. In his present capacity as official spokesman for the American Jewish Committee, the self-styled "Vatican of Judaism", Rabbi Morris N. Kertzer wrote a most revealing and comprehensive article with the title, "What is a Jew" which was published as a feature article in "Look" Magazine in the June 17, 1952 issue. In that article Rabbi Morris N. Kertzer evaluated the significance of the Talmud to "Judaism" today.

In that illuminating treatise on that important subject by the most qualified authority, at the time, Rabbi Morris N. Kertzer stated:

"The Talmud consists of 63 books of legal, ethical and historical writings of the ancient rabbis. It was edited five centuries after the birth of Jesus. It is a compendium of law and lore. IT IS THE LEGAL CODE WHICH FORMS THE BASIS OF JEWISH RELIGIOUS LAW AND IT IS THE TEXTBOOK USED IN THE TRAINING OF RABBIS." (emphasis supplied).

In view of this official evaluation of the importance of the Talmud in the practice of "Judaism" today by the highest body of so-called or self-styled "Jews" in the world it is very necessary at this time, my dear Dr. Goldstein, to inquire a little further into the subject of the Talmud. In his lifetime the eminent Michael Rodkinson, the assumed name of a so-called or self-styled "Jew" who was one of the world's great authorities on the Talmud, wrote "History of the Talmud." This great classic on the subject was written by Michael Rodkinson in collaboration with the celebrated Rabbi Isaac M. Wise. In his "History of the Talmud" Michael Rodkinson, on page 70, states:

"Is the literature that Jesus was familiar with in his early years yet in existence in the world? Is it possible for us to get at it? Can we ourselves review the ideas, the statements, the modes of reasoning and thinking, ON

MORAL AND RELIGIOUS SUBJECTS, which were current in his time, and MUST HAVE BEEN EVOLVED BY HIM DURING THOSE THIRTY SILENT YEARS WHEN HE WAS PONDERING HIS FUTURE MISSION? To such inquirers the learned class of Jewish rabbis ANSWER BY HOLDING UP THE TALMUD. Here, say they, is THE SOURCE FROM WHENCE JESUS OF NAZARETH DREW THE TEACHINGS WHICH ENABLED HIM TO REVOLUTIONIZE THE WORLD; and the question becomes, therefor, an interesting one TO EVERY CHRISTIAN. What is the Talmud? THE TALMUD, THEN, IS THE WRITTEN FORM OF THAT WHICH, IN THE TIME OF JESUS WAS CALLED THE TRADITION OF THE ELDERS AND TO WHICH HE MAKES FREQUENT ALLUSIONS. What sort of book is it? (emphasis supplied)

Stimulated by that invitation every Christian worthy of the name should immediately take the trouble to seek the answer to that "interesting" question "to every Christian". My dear Dr. Goldstein, your articles do not indicate whether you have taken the time and the trouble to personally investigate "what sort of book" the Talmud is either before or after your conversion to Catholicism. Have you ever done so? If you have done so what is the conclusion you have reached regarding "what sort of book" the Talmud is? What is your personal unbiased and unprejudiced opinion of the Talmud? Is it consistent with your present views as a devout Roman Catholic and a tried and true Christian? Can you spare a few moments to drop me a few lines on your present views?

In case you have never had the opportunity to investigate the contents of the "63 books" of the Talmud so well summarized by Rabbi Morris N. Kertzer in his illuminated article "What is a Jew", previously quoted, may I here impose upon your precious time to quote a few passages for you until you find the time to conveniently investigate the Talmud's contents personally. If I can be of any assistance to you in doing so please do not hesitate to let me know in what manner you can use my help.

From the birth of Jesus until this day there have never been recorded more vicious and vile libelous blasphemies of Jesus, or Christians and the Christian faith by anyone, anywhere or anytime than you will find between the covers of the infamous "63 books" which are "the legal code which forms the basis of Jewish religious law" as well as the "textbook used in the training of rabbis". The explicit and implicit irreligious character and implications of the contents of the Talmud will open your eyes as they have never been opened before. The Talmud reviles Jesus, Christians and the Christian faith as the priceless spiritual and cultural heritage of Christians has never been reviled before or since the Talmud was completed in the 5th century. You will have to excuse the foul, obscene, indecent, lewd and vile language you will see here as verbatim quotations from the official unabridged translation of the Talmud into English.

Be prepared for a surprise.

In the year 1935 the international hierarchy of so-called or self-styled "Jews" for the first time in history published an official unabridged translation of the complete Talmud in the English language with complete footnotes. What possessed them to make this translation into English is one of the unsolved mysteries. It was probably done because so many so-called or self-styled "Jews" of the younger generation were unable to read the Talmud in the many ancient languages in which the original "63 books" of the Talmud were first composed by their authors in many lands between 200 B.C. and 500 A.D.

The international hierarchy of so-called or self-styled "Jews" selected the most learned scholars to make this official translation of the Talmud into English. These famous scholars also prepared official footnotes explaining unabridged translation of the Talmud into English where they were required. This official unabridged translation of the Talmud into English with the official footnotes was printed in London in 1935 by the Soncino Press. It has been always referred to as the Soncino Edition of the Talmud. A very limited number of the Soncino Edition were printed. They were not made available to any purchaser. The Soncino Edition of the Talmud is to be found in the Library of Congress and the New York Public Library. A set of the Soncino Edition of the Talmud has been available to me for many years. They have become rare "collector's items" by now.

The Soncino Edition of the Talmud with its footnotes is like a double-edged sword. It teaches the Talmud to countless millions of the younger generation of so-called or self-styled "Jews" who are not able to read the Talmud in the many ancient languages in which the Talmud was written by its authors between 200 B.C. and 500 A.D. It also teaches Christians what the Talmud has to say about Jesus, about Christians and about the Christian faith. Someday this is bound to back-fire. Christians will someday challenge the assertion that the Talmud is the "sort of book" from which Jesus allegedly "drew the teachings which enabled him to revolutionize the world" on "moral and religious subjects". The rumbling is already heard in places.

Verbatim quotations from the Soncino Edition of the Talmud are required to illustrate the enormity of the Talmud's iniquity. My comments with verbatim quotations will prove inadequate to do that. In spite of the low language I will of necessity therefore include in this letter to you, I have no compunctions in the matter because the United States Post Office authorities do not bar the Soncino Edition of the Talmud from the mails. Nevertheless I apologize in advance for the language which will of necessity appear in this letter to you. You now understand.

The official unabridged Soncino Edition of the Talmud published in 1935 was "Translated into English with Notes, Glossary and Indices" by such eminent Talmudic scholars as Rabbi Dr. I. Epstein, Rabbi Dr. Samuel Daiches, Rabbi Dr. Israel W. Slotki, M.A., Litt.D., The Reverend Dr. A. Cohen, M.A.', Ph.D., Maurice Simon, M.A., and the Very Reverend The Chief Rabbi Dr. J.H. Hertz wrote the "Foreword" for the Soncino Edition of the Talmud. The Very Reverend Rabbi Hertz was at the time the Chief Rabbi of England.

The following are but a few of the many similar quotations with footnotes from the Soncino Edition of the Talmud, the "sort of book" from which Jesus allegedly "drew the teachings which enabled him to revolutionize the world" on "moral and religious" subjects:

*(Book)*

*SANHEDRIN, 55b-55a*: "What is meant by this? - Rab said: Pederasty with a child below nine years of age is not deemed as pederasty with a child above that. Samuel said: Pederasty with a child below three years is not treated as with a child above that (2) What is the basis of their dispute? - Rab maintains that only he who is able to engage in sexual intercourse, may, as the passive subject of pederasty throw guilty (upon the actual offender); whilst he who is unable to engage in sexual intercourse cannot be a passive subject of pederasty (in that respect) (3). But Samuel maintains: Scriptures writes, (And thou shalt not lie with mankind) as with the lyings of a woman (4). It has been taught in accordance with Rab: Pederasty at the age of nine years and a day; (55a) (he) who commits bestiality, whether naturally or unnaturally: or a woman who causes herself to be beastially abused, whether naturally or unnaturally, is liable to punishment (5)."

(footnotes)

(1) The reference is to the passive subject of sodomy. As stated in supra 54a, guilt is incurred by the active participant even if the former be a minor; i.e., less than thirteen years old. Now, however, it is stated that within this age a distinction is drawn.

(2) Rab makes nine years the minimum; but if one committed sodomy with a child of lesser age, no guilt is incurred. Samuel makes three the minimum.

(3) At nine years a male attains sexual matureness.

(4) Lev XVIII, 22

(5) Rashi reads ("xxx") (Hebrew characters, Ed.) instead of ("zzz") (Hebrew characters, Ed.) in our printed texts. A male, aged nine years and a day, who

commits etc. There are thus three distinct clauses in this Baraitha. The first a male aged nine years and a day - refers to the passive subject of pederasty, the punishment being incurred by the adult offender. This must be its meaning: because firstly, the active offender is never explicitly designated as a male, it being understood, just as the Bible states, Thou shalt not lie with mankind, where only the sex of the passive participant is mentioned; and secondly, if the age reference is to the active party, the guilt being incurred by the passive adult party, why single out pederasty: in all crimes of incest, the passive adult does not incur guilt unless the other party is at least nine years and a day? Hence the Baraitha supports Rab's contention that nine years (and a day) is the minimum age of the passive partner for the adult to be liable." (emphasis in original, Ed.)

Before giving any more verbatim quotations from the "sort of book" from which it is falsely alleged Jesus "drew the teachings which enabled him to revolutionize the world" on "moral and religious subjects" I wish to here again recall to your attention the official statement by Rabbi Morris N. Kertzer in `Look' Magazine for June 17, 1952. In that official statement made by Rabbi Morris N. Kertzer on behalf of The American Jewish Committee, self-styled "The Vatican of Judaism", informed the 20,000,000 readers of "Look' magazine that the Talmud "IS THE LEGAL CODE WHICH FORMS THE BASIS OF JEWISH RELIGIOUS LAW AND IT IS THE TEXTBOOK USED IN THE TRAINING OF RABBIS". Please bear this in mind as you read further.

Before continuing I wish also to call your attention to another feature. Confirming the official view of Rabbi Morris N. Kertzer, the *New York Times* on May 20, 1954 ran a news item under the headline "Rabbis Plan a Fund to Endow Two Chairs". The news item itself ran as follows: "Special to the New York Times, Uniontown, Pa. May 19 - Plans for raising $500,000, for the creation of two endowed chairs at the `Jewish Theological Seminary of America' were announced today at the fifty-fourth annual convention of the `Rabbinical Assembly of America'. THE PROFESSORSHIPS WOULD BE KNOWN AS THE LOUIS GINSBERG CHAIR IN TALMUD..."

This is further proof that the Talmud is not yet quite a dead-letter in the "TRAINING OF RABBIS". Is further proof needed on that question?

The world's leading authorities on the Talmud confirm that the official unabridged Soncino Edition of the Talmud translated into English follows the original texts with great exactness. It is almost a word-for-word translation of the original texts. In his famous classic "The History of the Talmud Michael Rodkinson, the leading authority on the Talmud, in collaboration with the celebrated Reverend Dr. Isaac M. Wise states:

With the conclusion of the first volume of this work at the beginning of the twentieth century, we would invite the reader to take a glance over the past of the Talmud, in which he will see... that not only was the Talmud not destroyed, but was so saved that NOT A SINGLE LETTER OF IT IS MISSING; and now IT IS FLOURISHING TO SUCH A DEGREE AS CANNOT BE FOUND IN ITS PAST HISTORY...THE TALMUD IS ONE OF THE WONDERS OF THE WORLD. During the twenty centuries of its existence...IT SURVIVED IN ITS ENTIRETY, and not only has the power of its foes FAILED TO DESTROY EVEN A SINGLE LINE, but it has not even been able materially to weaken its influence for any length of time. IT STILL DOMINATES THE MINDS OF A WHOLE PEOPLE, WHO VENERATE ITS CONTENTS AS DIVINE TRUTH... The colleges for the study of the Talmud are increasing almost in every place where Israel dwells, especially in this country where millions are gathered for the funds of the two colleges, the Hebrew Union College of Cincinnati and the Jewish Theological Seminary of America in New York, in which the chief study is the Talmud... There are also in our city houses of learning (Jeshibath) for the study of the Talmud in the lower East Side, where many young men are studying the Talmud every day."

This "divine truth" which "a whole people venerate" of which "not a single letter of it is missing" and today "is flourishing  to such a degree as cannot be found in its history" is illustrated by the additional verbatim quotations which follow:


*(Book)*

*SANHEDRIN, 55b:* "A maiden three years and a day may be acquired in marriage by coition, and if her deceased husband's brother cohabits with her, she becomes his. The penalty of adultery may be incurred through her; (if a niddah) she defiles him who has connection with her, so that he in turn defiles that upon which he lies, as a garment which has lain upon (a person afflicted with gonorrhea)." (emphasis in original text of Soncino Edition, Ed.)


(footnotes)

(2) His wife derives no pleasure from this, and hence there is no cleaving.

(3) A variant reading of this passage is: Is there anything permitted to a Jew which is forbidden to a heathen. Unnatural connection is permitted to a Jew.

(4) By taking the two in conjunction, the latter as illustrating the former, we learn that the guilt of violating the injunction `to his wife but not to his neighbor's wife' is incurred only for natural but not for unnatural intercourse."

(emphasis in original, Ed.)


*(Book)*

*SANHEDRIN, 69a* " `A man'; from this I know the law only with respect to a man: whence do I know it of one aged nine years and a day who is capable of intercourse? From the verse, And `if a man'? (2) He replied: Such a minor can produce semen, but cannot beget therewith; for it is like the seed of cereals less than a third grown (3)."


(footnotes)

(2) `And' (`) indicates an extension of the law, and is here interpreted to include a minor aged nine years and a day.

(3) Such cereals contain seed, which if sown, however, will not grow."


*(Book)*

*SANHEDRIN, 69b* "Our rabbis taught: If a woman sported lewdly with her young son (a minor), and he committed the first stage of cohabitation with her, - Beth Shammai say, he thereby renders her unfit for the priesthood (1). Beth Hillel declare her fit...All agree that the connection of a boy nine years and a day is a real connection; whilst that of one less than eight years is not (2); their dispute refers only to one who is eight years old.


(footnotes) (1) i.e., she becomes a harlot whom a priest may not marry (Lev XXL,7.). (2) so that if he was nine years and a day or more, Beth Hillel agree that she is invalidated from the priesthood; whilst if he was less than eight, Beth Shammai agree that she is not."


*(Book)*

*KETHUBOTH, 5b.* "The question was asked: Is it allowed (15) to perform the first marital act on the Sabbath? (16). Is the blood (in the womb) stored up (17), or is it the result of a wound? (18).


(footnotes) "(15) Lit., `how is it'? (16) When the intercourse could not take place before the Sabbath (Tosaf) (17) And the intercourse would be allowed, since the blood flows out of its own accord, no would having been made. (18) Lit., or is it wounded? And the intercourse would be forbidden."

*(Book)*

*KETHUBOTH, 10a-10b.* "Someone came before Rabban Gamaliel the son of Rabbi (and) said to him, `my master I have had intercourse (with my newly wedded wife) and I have not found any blood (7). She (the wife) to him, `My master, I am still a virgin'. He (then) said to them; Bring me two handmaids, one (who is) a virgin and one who had intercourse with a man. They brought to him (two such handmaids), and he placed them on a cask of wine. (In the case of ) the one  who was no more a virgin its smell (1) went through (2), (in the case of) the virgin the smell did not go through (3). He (then) placed this one (the young wife) also (on the cask of wine), and its smell (4) did not go through. He (then) said to him: Go, be happy with thy bargain (7). But he should have examined her from the beginning (8)."

(footnotes)

(1) i.e., the smell of wine.

(2) One could smell the wine from the mouth (Rashi).

(3) One could not smell the wine from the mouth.

(4) i.e., the smell of wine.

(5) Rabban Gamaliel

(6) To the husband.

(7) The test showed that the wife was a virgin.

(8) Why did he first have to experiment with the two handmaids.

*(Book)*

*KETHUBOTH, 11a-11b.* "Rabba said, It means (5) this: When a grown up man has intercourse with a little girl it is nothing, for when the girl is less than this (6), it is as if one puts the finger in the eye (7), but when a small boy has intercourse with a grown up woman, he makes her as `a girl who is injured by a piece of wood' ".

(footnotes)

(5). Lit., `says'.

(6) Lit., `here', that is, less than three years old.

(7) Tears come to the eyes again and again, so does virginity come back to the little girl under three years.

*(Book)*

KETHUBOTH, 11a-11b. "Rab Judah said that Rab said: A small boy who has intercourse with a grown up woman makes her (as though she were ) injured by a piece of wood (1). Although the intercourse of a small boy is not regarded as a sexual act, nevertheless the woman is injured by it as by a piece of wood."

(footnotes)

(1) Although the intercourse of a small boy is not regarded as a sexual act, nevertheless the woman is injured by it as by a piece of wood.

*(Book)*

HAYORATH, 4a. "We learnt: (THE LAW CONCERNING THE MENSTRUANT OCCURS IN THE TORAH BUT IF A MAN HAS INTERCOURSE WITH A WOMAN THAT AWAITS A DAY CORRESPONDING TO A DAY HE IS EXEMPT. But why?

Surely (the law concerning) a woman that awaits a day corresponding to a day is mentioned in the Scriptures: He hath made naked her fountain. But, surely it is written, (1)- They might rule that in the natural way even the first stage of contact is forbidden; and in an unnatural way, however, is (that the ruling might have been permitted) (3) even in the natural way (4) alleging (that the prohibition of) the first stage (5) has reference to a menstruant woman only (6). And if you prefer I might say: The ruling may have been that a woman is not regarded as a zabah (7) except during the daytime because it is written, all the days of her issue (8)." (emphasis appears in Soncino Edition original, Ed.)

(footnotes)

(13) Lev. XV, 28.

(14) Cf. supra p. 17, n. 10. Since she is thus Biblically considered unclean how

could a court rule that one having intercourse with her is exempt?

(15) Lev XX, 18.

(1) Ibid. 13. The plural "xxxx" (Hebrew characters, Ed.) implies natural, and unnatural intercourse.

(2) Why then was the case of `a woman who awaits a day corresponding to a day' given as an illustration when the case of a menstruant, already mentioned, would apply the same illustration.

(3) The first stage of contact.

(4) In the case of one `who awaits a day corresponding to a day'; only consummation of coition being forbidden in her case.

(5) Cf. Lev XX, 18.

(6) Thus permitting a forbidden act which the Sadducees do not admit.

(7) A woman who has an issue of blood not in the time of her menstruation, and is subject to certain laws of uncleanness and purification (Lev XV, 25ff).

(8) Lev XV, 26. Emphasis being laid on days.


*(Book)*

*ABODAH ZARAH, 36b-37a.* "R. Naham B. Isaac said: They decreed in connection with a heathen child that it would cause defilement by seminal emission (2) so that an Israelite child should not become accustomed to commit pederasty with it...From what age does a heathen child cause defilement by seminal emission? From the age of nine years and one day. (37a) for inasmuch as he is then capable of the sexual act he likewise defiles by emission. Rabina said: It is therefore to be concluded that a heathen girl (communicates defilement) from the age of three years and one day, for inasmuch as she is then capable of the sexual act she likewise defiles by a flux.


(footnotes)

(2). Even though he suffered from no issue.


*(Book)*

*SOTAH, 26b.* "R. Papa said: It excludes an animal, because there is not adultery in connection with an animal (4). Raba of Parazika (5) asked R. Ashi, Whence is the statement which the Rabbis made that there is no adultery in connection with an animal? Because it is written, Thou shalt not bring the hire of a harlot or the wages of a dog etc.; (6) and it has been taught: The hire of a dog (7) and the wages of a harlot (8) are permissible, as it is said, even both of these (9) - the two (specified texts are abominations) but not four (10)...As lying with mankind. (12) But, said Raba, it excludes the case where he warned her against contact of the bodies (13). Abaye said to him, That is merely an obscene act (and not adultery), and did the All-Merciful prohibit (a wife to her husband) for an obscene act?" (emphasis in the original text, Ed.)

(footnotes)

(4) She would not be prohibited to her husband for such an act.

(5) farausag near Baghdad v. BB. (Sonc. Ed.) p. 15, n.4. He is thus distinguished from the earlier Rabbi of that name.

(6) Deut. XXIII, 19.

(7) Money given by a man to a harlot to associate with his dog. Such an association is not legal adultery.

(8) If a man had a female slave who was a harlot and he exchanged her for an animal, it could be offered.

(9) Are an abomination unto the Lord (ibid).

(10) Viz., the other two mentioned by the Rabbi.

(11) In Num. V. 13. since the law applies to a man who is incapable.

(12) Lev. XVIII, 22. The word for `lying' is in the plural and is explained as denoting also unnatural intercourse.

(13) With the other man, although there is no actual coition." (emphasis appears in original Soncino Edition, Ed.)

*(Book)*

*YEBAMOTH, 55b.* "Raba said; for what purpose did the All-Merciful write `carnally' in connection with the designated bondmaid (9), a married woman (10) and a sotah? (11) That in connection with the designated bondmaid (is required) as has just been explained (12). That in connection with a married woman excludes intercourse with a relaxed membrum (13). This is a satisfactory interpretation in accordance with the view of him who maintains that if one cohabited with forbidden relatives with relaxed membrum he is exonerated (14); what, however, can be said, according to him who maintains (that for such an act one is) guilty? The exclusion is rather that of intercourse with a dead woman (15). Since it might have been assumed that, as (a wife), even after her death, is described as his kin (16), one should be guilty for (intercourse with) her (as for that) with a married woman, hence we are taught (that one is exonerated).

(footnotes)

(9) Lev. XIX,20.

(10) Ibid. XVIII,20

(11) Num. V, 13.

(12) SUPRA 55a.

(13) Since no fertilization can possibly occur.

(14) Shebu., 18a, Sanh. 55a

(15) Even though she dies as a married woman.

(16) In Lev. XXI, 2. where the text enumerates the dead relatives for whom a priest may defile himself. As was explained, *supra* 22b, *his kin* refers to one's wife. (emphasis in Soncino Edition original, Ed.)

*(Book)*

*YEBAMOTH, 103a-103b.* "When the serpent copulated with Eve (14) with lust. The lust of the Israelites who stood at Mount Sinai (16) came to an end, the lust of idolaters who did not stand at Mount Sinai did not come to an end."

(footnotes)

(14) In the Garden of Eden, according to tradition.

(15) i.e., the human species.

(16) And experienced the purifying influence of divine Revelation."

*(Book)*

*YEBAMOTH, 63a.* "R. Eleazar further stated: What is meant by the Scriptural text, This is now bone of my bones, and flesh of my flesh (5)? This teaches that Adam had intercourse with every beast and animal but found no satisfaction until he cohabited with Eve.

(5) Gen. II, 23. emphasis on This is now." (emphasis appears in original Sonsino Edition, Ed.)

*(Book)*

*YEBAMOTH, 60b.* "As R. Joshua b. Levi related: `There was a certain town in the Land of Israel the legitimacy of whose inhabitants was disputed, and Rabbi sent R. Ramanos who conducted an inquiry and found in it the daughter of a proselyte who was under the age of three years and one day (14), and Rabbi declared her eligible to live with a priest (15)."

(13) A proselyte under the age of three years and one day may be married by a priest.

(14) And was married to a priest.

(15) i.e., permitted to continue to live with her husband."

*(Book)*

*YEBAMOTH, 59b.* "R. Shimi b. Hiyya stated: A woman who had intercourse with a beast is eligible to marry a priest (4). Likewise it was taught: A woman who had intercourse with that which is no human being (5), though she is in consequence subject to the penalty of stoning (6), is nevertheless permitted to marry a priest (7).

(4) Even a High Priest. The result of such intercourse being regarded as a mere wound, and the opinion that does not regard an accidentally injured hymen as a disqualification does not so regard such an intercourse either.

(5) A beast.

(6) If the offense was committed in the presence of witnesses after due warning.

(7) In the absence of witnesses and warning."

*(Book)*

YEBAMOTH, 12b "R. Bebai recited before R. Naham: Three (categories of) woman may (7) use an absorbent (8) in their marital intercourse (9), a minor, a pregnant woman and a nursing woman. The minor (10) because (otherwise) she might (11) become pregnant, and as a result (11) might die...And what is the age of such a minor? (14). From the age of eleven years and one day until the age of twelve years and one day. One who is under (15), or over this age (16) must carry on her marital intercourse in the usual manner."


(footnotes)

(7) (so Rashi. R. Tam; Should use, v.Tosaf s.v.)

(8) Hackled wool or flax

(9) To prevent conception

(10) May use an absorbent.

(11) Lit., `perhaps'.

(14) Who is capable of conception but exposed thereby to the danger of death.

(15) When no conception is possible.

(16) When pregnancy involves no fatal consequences."


*(Book)*

YEBAMOTH, 59b. "When R. Dimi came (8) he related: It once happened at Haitalu (9) that while a young woman was sweeping the floor (10) a village dog (11) covered her from the rear (12) and Rabbi permitted her to marry a priest. Samuel said: Even a High Priest.


(footnotes)

(8) From Palestine to Babylon

(9) (Babylonian form for Aitulu, modern Aiterun N.W. of Kadesh, v. S. Klein, Beitrage, p. 47).

(10) Lit., `house'.

(11) Or `big hunting dog' (Rashi), `ferocious dog' (Jast.), `small wild dog' (Aruk).

(12) A case of unnatural intercourse.


*(Book)*

*KETHUBOTH, 6b.* "Said he to him: Not like those Babylonians who are not skilled in moving aside. (7), but there are some who are skilled in moving aside (8). If so, why (give the reason of) `anxious.? (10) for one who is not skilled. (Then) let the[m] say: One who is skilled is allowed (to perform the first intercourse on Sabbath), one who is not skilled is forbidden? Most (people) are skilled (11). Said Raba the son of R. Hanan to Abaye' If this were so, then why (have) groomsmen (12) why (have) a sheet? (13) He - (Abaye) said to him: There (the groomsmen and the sheet are necessary) perhaps he will see and destroy (the tokens of her virginity) (14)."


(footnotes)

(7) i.e., having intercourse with a virgin without causing a bleeding.

(8) Thus no blood need come out, and `Let his head be cut off and let him not die!' does not apply.

(9) If the bridegroom is skilled in `moving sideways'.

(10) He need not be anxious about the intercourse and should not be free from reading Shema' on account of such anxiety.

(11) Therefore the principle regarding `Let his head be cut off and let him not die!' does not, as a rule, apply.

(12) The groomsmen testify in case of need to the virginity of the bride. V. *infra* 12a. If the bridegroom will act in a manner that will cause no bleeding, the groomsmen will not be able to testify on the question of virginity.

(13) To provide evidence of the virginity of the bride. Cf. Deut. XXII, 17.

(14) It may happen that he will act in the normal manner and cause bleeding but he will destroy the tokens and maintain that the bride was not a virgin; for this reason the above mentioned provisions are necessary. Where however he moved aside and made a false charge as to her virginity, the bride can plead that she is still a virgin (Rashi)."


After reading these verbatim quotations from the countless other similar quotations which you will find in the official unabridged Soncino Edition of the Talmud in the English language are you of the opinion, my dear Dr. Goldstein, that the Talmud was the "sort of book" from which Jesus "drew the teachings which enabled him to revolutionize the world" on "moral and religious subjects"? You have read here verbatim quotations and official footnotes on a few of the many other subjects covered by the "63 books" of the Talmud. When you read them you must be prepared for a shock. I am surprised that the United States Post Office does not bar the Talmud from the mails. I hesitate to quote them in this letter.

In support of the contention by the top echelon among the outstanding authorities on this phase of the present status of the Talmud, further proof of the wide influence exerted by the Talmud upon the so-called or self-styled "Jews" is supplied by Rabbi Morris N. Kertzer's article "What is a Jew" in the June 17, 1952 issue of `Look Magazine'. Rabbi Morris N. Kertzer's article contains a lovely picture of a smiling man seated in a chair with a large opened book upon his lap. Seated around him on the floor are about a dozen smiling men and women.

They are paying close attention to the smiling man in the chair with the opened book upon his lap. He is reading to the persons on the floor. He emphasizes what he is reading by gestures with one of his hands. Beneath this photograph of the group is the following explanation:

"ADULTS STUDY ANCIENT WRITINGS TOO. RABBI, IN THIS PICTURE, SEATED IN CHAIR, LEADS GROUP DISCUSSION OF TALMUD BEFORE EVENING PRAYER." (emphasis supplied)

This picture and explanation indicate the extent the Talmud is the daily diet of so-called or self-styled "Jews" in this day and age. The Talmud is first taught to children of so-called or self- styled "Jews" as soon as they are able to read. Just as the Talmud is the "textbook by which rabbis are trained" so is the Talmud also the textbook by which the rank-and-file of the so-called or self-styled "Jews" are "trained" to think from their earliest age. In the translation of the Talmud with its texts edited, corrected and formulated by the eminent Michael Rodkinson, with its first edition revised and corrected by the celebrated Reverend Dr. Isaac M. Wise, on page XI, it states:

"THE MODERN JEW IS THE PRODUCT OF THE TALMUD"

(emphasis supplied)


To the average Christian the word "Talmud" is just another word associated by them with the form of religious worship practiced in their synagogues by so-called or self-styled "Jews". Many Christians have never heard of the Talmud.

Very few Christians are informed on the contents of the Talmud. Some may believe the Talmud to be an integral part of the religious worship known to them as "Judaism". It suggests a sort of bible or religious text book. It is classed as a spiritual manual. But otherwise few if any Christians have an understanding of the contents of the Talmud and what it means in the daily lives of so-called or self-styled "Jews". As an illustration, my dear Dr. Goldstein, how many Christians have any conception of the "Kol Nidre" (All Vows) prayer recited in synagogues on the Day of Atonement?

In Volume VIII of the Jewish Encyclopedia on page 539 found in the Library of Congress, the New York Public Library and libraries of all leading cities, will be found the official translation into English of the prayer known as the "Kol Nidre" (All Vows) prayer. It is the prologue of the Day of Atonement services in the synagogues. IT is recited three times by the standing congregation in concert with chanting rabbis at the alter. After the recital of the "Kol Nidre" (All Vows) prayer the Day of Atonement religious ceremonies follow immediately. The Day of Atonement religious observances are the highest holy days of the so-called or self-styled "Jews" and are celebrated as such throughout the world. The official translation into English of the "Kol Nidre" (All Vows) prayer follows:

"ALL VOWS, OBLIGATIONS, OATHS, ANATHEMAS, whether called `konam', `konas', or by any other name, WHICH WE MAY VOW, OR SWEAR, OR PLEDGE, OR WHEREBY WE MAY BE BOUND, FROM THIS DAY OF ATONEMENT UNTO THE NEXT, (whose happy coming we await), we do repent. MAY THEY BE DEEMED ABSOLVED, FORGIVEN, ANNULLED, AND VOID AND MADE OF NO EFFECT; THEY SHALL NOT BIND US NOR HAVE POWERS OVER US. THE VOWS SHALL NOT BE RECKONED VOWS; THE OBLIGATIONS SHALL NOT BE OBLIGATORY; NOR THE OATHS BE OATHS."
(emphasis supplied)


The implications, inferences and innuendoes of the "Kol Nidre" (All Vows) prayer are referred to in the Talmud in the Book of Nedarim, 23a-23b as follows:


*(Book)*

"And he who desires that NONE OF HIS VOWS MADE DURING THE YEAR SHALL BE VALID, let him stand at the beginning of the year and declare, `EVERY VOW WHICH I MAKE IN THE FUTURE SHALL BE NULL (1). (HIS VOWS ARE THEN INVALID,) PROVIDING THAT HE

REMEMBERS THIS AT THE TIME OF THE VOW." (emphasis in original and supplied, Ed.)


(footnotes)

(1) This may have provided a support for the custom of reciting Kol Nidre (a formula for dispensation of vows) prior to the Evening Service of the Day of Atonement (Ran)...Though the beginning of the year (New Year) is mentioned here, the Day of Atonement was probably chosen on account of its great solemnity. But Kol Nidre as part of the ritual IS LATER THAN THE TALMUD, and, as seen from the following statement of R. Huna b. Hinene, THE LAW OF REVOCATION IN ADVANCE WAS NOT MADE PUBLIC. (emphasis supplied and in original text, Ed.)


The greatest study of the "Kol Nidre" (all Vows) prayer was made by the eminent psycho-analyst Professor Theodor Reik, the celebrated pupil of the famous Dr. Sigmund Freud. The analysis of the historic, religious and psychological background of the "Kol Nidre" (All Vows) prayer by Professor Reik presents the Talmud in its true perspective. This important study is contained in Professor Reik's "The Ritual, Psycho-Analytical Studies". In the chapter on the Talmud, on page 168, Professor Reik states:

"THE TEXT WAS TO THE EFFECT THAT ALL OATHS WHICH BELIEVERS TAKE BETWEEN ONE DAY OF ATONEMENT AND THE NEXT DAY OF ATONEMENT ARE DECLARED INVALID." (emphasis added)

Before explaining to you how the present wording of the "Kol Nidre" (All Vows) prayer was introduced into the Day of Atonement synagogue ceremonies, my dear Dr. Goldstein, I would like to quote a passage to you from the Universal Jewish Encyclopedia. The Universal Jewish Encyclopedia confirms the fact that the "Kol Nidre" (All Vows) prayer has no spiritual value as might be believed because it is recited in synagogues on the Day of Atonement as the prologue of the religious ceremonies which follow it. The secular significance of the "Kol Nidre" (All Vows) prayer is indicated forcefully by the analysis in the Universal Jewish Encyclopedia. In Volume VI, on page 441, it states:

"The Kol Nidre HAS NOTHING WHATEVER TO DO WITH THE ACTUAL IDEA OF THE DAY OF ATONEMENT...it attained to extraordinary solemnity and popularity by reason of the fact that it was THE FIRST PRAYER RECITED ON THIS HOLIEST OF DAYS."

My dear Dr. Goldstein, prepare for the shock of your life. Compelled by what you may now read here about the "Kol Nidre" (All Vows) prayer you must be shocked to learn that many Christian churches actually "peal their bells" on the Day of Atonement in celebration of that holy day for so-called or self-styled "Jews." How stupid can the Christian clergy get? From what I have learned after a cursory inquiry I am unable to say whether it was a case of stupidity or cupidity. With what you already know, together with what [you] will additionally know before you finish this letter, you will be able to judge for yourself whether it was stupidity or cupidity. There is not one single fact in this entire letter which every graduate of a theological seminary did not have the opportunity to learn.

The following news item was featured in the New York `World Telegram' on October 7th only a few days ago. Under a prominent headline "JEWISH HOLIDAYS TO END AT SUNDOWN" the New York `World Telegram' gave great prominence to the following story:

"Synagogues and temples throughout the city were crowded yesterday as the 24 hour fast began. Dr. Normal Salit, head of the Synagogue Council of America, representing the three major Jewish bodies, had called on other faiths TO JOIN THE FAST... Cutting across religious lines, MANY PROTESTANT CHURCHES IN THE CITY PEALED THEIR BELLS LAST NIGHT TO SOUND THE KOL NIDRE, TRADITIONAL MELODY USED AT THE START OF YOM KIPPUR. THE GESTURE OF GOOD-WILL WAS RECOMMENDED BY THE MANHATTAN OFFICE OF THE PROTESTANT COUNCIL" (emphasis supplied).

That just about "tops" anything I have ever had come to my attention revealing the ignorance and indifference of the Christian clergy to the hazards today facing the Christian faith. From my personal contacts with the Manhattan Office of the Protestant Council in the recent past I hold out very little hope for any constructive contribution they can make to the common defense of the Christian faith against its dedicated enemies. In each instance they buckled under the "pressure" exerted upon them by the "contacts" for so-called or self-styled "Jews". If it was not so tragic it would be comic. It was a joke indeed but the joke was on the Christian clergy. Ye Gods! "Many" Christian churches "pealed their bells", as the Protestant Council reports the event, "TO SOUND THE KOL NIDRE, TRADITIONAL MELODY USED AT THE START OF YOM KIPPUR". Just where does betrayal of a trust and breach of faith begin?

The present wording of the "Kol Nidre" (All Vows) prayer dates from the 11th century. A political reversal in Eastern Europe compelled the so-called or self-styled "Jews" in eastern Europe to adopt the present wording of the "Kol

Nidre" (All Vows) prayer. That story involves the history of the so-called or self-styled "Jews". Before relating here as briefly as possible the history of the so-called or self-styled "Jews" of eastern Europe I would like to quote here another short passage from the Jewish Encyclopedia. In analyzing the course of history which resulted in the present wording of the "Kol Nidre" (All Vows) prayer the Jewish Encyclopedia in Volume VII, on page 540, states:

"AN IMPORTANT ALTERATION IN THE WORDING of the `Kol Nidre' was made by Rashi's son-in-law, Meir ben Samuel, WHO CHANGED THE ORIGINAL PHRASE `FROM THE LAST DAY OF ATONEMENT TO THIS ONE' to `FROM THIS DAY OF ATONEMENT UNTIL THE NEXT' ". (emphasis supplied)

You will agree, my dear Dr. Goldstein, that Meir ben Samuel knew what he was doing. The wording of that altered version of the "Kol Nidre" (All Vows) prayer makes the recital of the prayer a release during the coming year from any obligations to respect any oath, vow or pledge during the coming year. Like any one-year license obtained from the Federal, State or Municipal governments, the altered version of the "Kol Nidre" (All Vows) prayer extends immunity in advance for one year from all obligations to observe the terms of oaths, vows and pledges made in the year following the date of the Day of Atonement when the prayer was recited. Each year however it becomes necessary to renew this "license" which automatically revokes in advance any oath, vow or pledge made during the next twelve months, by again appearing in a synagogue on the next Day of Atonement and reciting the "Kol Nidre" (All Vows) prayer again. Do you approve of this?

The passage in the Talmud referring to "Kol Nidre" (All Vows) prayer certifies to several serious situations. It certifies that "Kol Nidre" (All Vows) prayer was added as a prologue to the Day of Atonement religious services long after the completion of the Talmud between 500 A.D. - 1000 A.D. by the statement, "as part of the ritual is later than the Talmud." It confirms that Meir ben Samuel who authored the present altered version of the "Kol Nidre" (All Vows) prayer lived in the 11th century. Furthermore, the so-called or self-styled "Jews" in eastern Europe believed it served their purpose better to keep secret from their Christian conquerors their attitude on oaths, vows and pledges, "the law of revocation in advance was not made public."

With a complete and accurate knowledge of the origin and history of the so-called or self-styled "Jews" in eastern Europe, my dear Dr. Goldstein, it is quite impossible for yourself or for anybody to intelligently understand the harmful influence the Talmud has exerted for ten centuries, and the "Kol Nidre" (All Vows) prayer for seven centuries upon the course of world history. These two little known factors are the hub and the spokes of the "big wheel" rolling merrily along the road to complete world domination in the not distant future, without arousing suspicion, and wearing the innocent disguise of an alleged religious belief as their only defense mechanism. This insidious intrigue creates a most effective camouflage for the conspirators. The virility of their plot presents a problem in the defense of the political, economic, social and cultural ideologies developed under a Christian civilization.

You will probably also be an astonished as the 150,000,000 Christians years ago when I electrified the nation with the first publication by me of the facts disclosed by my many years of research into the origin and the history of the so-called or self-styled "Jews" in eastern Europe. My many years of intensive research established beyond the question of any doubt, contrary to the generally accepted belief held by Christians, that the so-called or self-styled "Jews" in eastern Europe at any time in their history in eastern Europe were never the legendary "lost ten tribes" of Bible lore. That historic fact is incontrovertible.

Relentless research established as equally true that the so-called or self-styled "Jews" in eastern Europe at no time in their history could be correctly regarded as the direct lineal descendants of the legendary "lost ten tribes" of Bible lore. The so-called or self-styled "Jews" in Eastern Europe in modern history cannot legitimately point to a single ancient ancestor who ever set even a foot on the soil of Palestine in the era of Bible history. Research also revealed that the so-called or self-styled "Jews" in Eastern Europe were never "Semites", are not "Semites" now, nor can they ever be regarded as "Semites" at any future time by any stretch of the imagination. Exhaustive research also irrevocably rejects as a fantastic fabrication the generally accepted belief by Christians that the so-called or self-styled "Jews" in Eastern Europe are the legendary "Chosen People" so very vocally publicized by the Christian clergy form their pulpits.

Maybe you can explain to me, my dear Dr. Goldstein, the reason why and just how the origin and the history of the Khazars and Khazar Kingdom was so well concealed from the world for so many centuries? What secret mysterious power has been able for countless generations to keep the origin and the history of the Khazars and Khazar Kingdom out of history text-books and out of class-room courses in history throughout the world? The origin and history of the Khazars and Khazar Kingdom are certainly incontestable historical facts. These incontestable historic facts also establish beyond any question of doubt the origin and history of the so-called or self-styled "Jews" in Eastern Europe. The origin and history of the Khazars and Khazar kingdom and their relationship to the origin and early history of the so-called or self-styled "Jews" in Eastern Europe was one of history's best kept secrets until wide publicity was given in recent years to my research on this subject. Do you not think, my dear Dr. Goldstein, that it is time this whole subject was dragged out of its hiding place?

In the year 1948 in the Pentagon in Washington I addressed a large assembly of the highest ranking officers of the United States Army principally in the G2 branch of Military Intelligence on the highly explosive geopolitical situation in Eastern Europe and the Middle East. Then as now that area of the world was a potential threat to the peace of the world and to the security of this nation I explained to them fully the origin of the Khazars and Khazar Kingdom. I felt then as I feel now that without a clear and comprehensive knowledge of that subject it is not possible to understand or to evaluate properly what has been taking place in the world since 1917, the year of the Bolshevik revolution in Russia. It is the "key" to that problem.

Upon the conclusion of my talk a very alert Lieutenant Colonel present at the meeting informed me that he was the head of the history department of one of the largest and highest scholastic rated institutions of higher education in the United States. He had taught history there for 16 years. He had recently been called back to Washington for further military service. To my astonishment he informed me that he had never in all his career as a history teachers or otherwise heard the word "khazar" before he heard me mention it there. That must give you some idea, my dear Dr. Goldstein, of how successful that mysterious secret power was with their plot to "block out" the origin and the history of the Khazars and Khazar Kingdom in order to conceal from the world and particularly Christians the true origin and the history of the so-called or self-styled "Jews" in eastern Europe.

The Russian conquest in the 10th-13th centuries of the little-known-to-history Khazars apparently ended the existence for all time of the little-known-to-history 800,000 square mile sovereign kingdom of the so-called or self-styled "Jews" in Eastern Europe, known then as the Khazar Kingdom. Historians and theologians now agree that this political development was the reason for the "IMPORTANT CHANGE IN THE WORDING OF THE 'KOL NIDRE' by Meir ben Samuel in the 11th century, and for the policy adopted by the so-called or self-styled "Jews" that "THE LAW OF REVOCATION IN ADVANCE WAS NOT MADE PUBLIC". Will you be patient with me while I review here as briefly as I can the history of that political emergence and disappearance of a nation from the pages of history?

Prior to the 10th century the Khazar Kingdom had already been reduced by Russian conquests to an area of about 800,000 square miles. As you can see on the map from the Jewish Encyclopedia [Reproduced in the book form of this tract, "Facts are Facts"] the territory of the Khazar Kingdom in the 10th century was still by far the largest of any nation in Europe. The population of the Khazar Kingdom was made up for the most part of Khazars with the addition of the remnants of the populations of the 25 peaceful agricultural nations which had inhabited this approximately 1,000,000 square miles before their conquest by the invading Khazars. In the 1st century B.C. the Khazars had invaded eastern Europe from their homeland in Asia. The Khazars invaded eastern Europe via the land route between the north end of the Caspian Sea and the south end of the Ural Mountains. (see map.)

The Khazars were not "Semites". They were an Asiatic Mongoloid nation. They are classified by modern anthropologists as Turco-Finns racially. From time immemorial the homeland of the Khazars was in the heart of Asia. They were a very warlike nation. The Khazars were driven out of Asia finally by the nations in Asia with whom they were continually at war. The Khazars invaded Eastern Europe to escape further defeats in Asia. The very warlike Khazars did not find it difficult to subdue and conquer the 25 peaceful agricultural nations occupying approximately 1,000,000 square miles in Eastern Europe. In a comparatively short period the Khazars established the largest and most powerful kingdom in Europe, and probably the wealthiest also.

The Khazars were a pagan nation when they invaded Eastern Europe. Their religious worship was a mixture of phallic worship and other forms of idolatrous worship practiced in Asia by pagan nations. This form of worship continued until the 7th century. The vile forms of sexual excess indulged in by the Khazars as their form of religious worship produced a degree of moral degeneracy the Khazar's king could not endure. In the 7th century King Bulan, ruler at that time of the Khazar Kingdom, decided to abolish the practice of phallic worship and other forms of idolatrous worship and make one of the three monotheistic religions, about which he knew very little, the new state religion. After a historic session with representatives of the three monotheistic religions King Bulan decided against Christian and Islam and selected as the future state religion as the religious worship then known as "Talmudism", and now known and practiced as "Judaism". This even is well documented in history.

King Bulan and his 4000 feudal nobles were promptly converted by rabbis imported from Babylonia for that event. Phallic worship and other forms of idolatry were thereafter forbidden. The Khazar kings invited large numbers of rabbis to come and open synagogues and schools to instruct the population in the new form of religious worship. It was now the state religion. The converted Khazars were the first population of so-called or self-styled "Jews" in Eastern Europe. So-called or self-styled "Jews" in Eastern Europe after the conversion of the Khazars the descendants of the Khazars converted to "Talmudism", or as it is now know "Judaism", by the 7th century mass conversion of the Khazar population.

After the conversion of King Bulan none but a so-called or self-styled "Jew" could occupy the Khazar throne. The Khazar Kingdom became a virtual theocracy. The religious leaders were the civil administrators also. The religious leaders imposed the teachings of the Talmud upon the population as their guide to living. The ideologies of the Talmud became the axis of political, cultural, economic and social attitudes and activities throughout the Khazar kingdom. The Talmud provided civil and religious law.

It might be very interesting for you, my dear Dr. Goldstein, if you have the patience, to allow me to quote for you here form Volume IV, pages 1 to 5, of the Jewish Encyclopedia. The Jewish Encyclopedia refers to the Khazars as "Chazars". The two spellings are optional according to the best authorities. The two are pronounced alike. Either Khazar or "Chazar" is pronounced like the first syllable of "costume" with the word "Czar" added onto it. It is correctly pronounced "cos(tume)Czar". The Jewish Encyclopedia has five pages on the Khazars but I will skip through them:

"CHAZARS: A people of Turkish origin whose life and history are interwoven with THE VERY BEGINNINGS OF THE HISTORY OF THE JEWS OF RUSSIA ... driven on by the nomadic tribes of the steppes and by THEIR OWN DESIRE FOR PLUNDER AND REVENGE ...

In the second half of the sixth century the Chazars moved westward...The kingdom of the Chazars was firmly established in MOST OF SOUTH RUSSIA LONG BEFORE THE FOUNDATIONS OF THE RUSSIAN MONARCHY BY THE VARANGIAN (855) ... At this time the kingdom of the Chazars stood at the height of its power AND WAS CONSTANTLY AT WAR ... At the end of the eighth century ... the chagan (king) of the Chazars and his grandees, TOGETHER WITH A LARGE NUMBER OF HIS HEATHEN PEOPLE, EMBRACED THE JEWISH RELIGION ...

The Jewish population in the entire domain of the Chazars, in the period between the seventh and tenth centuries, MUST HAVE BEEN CONSIDERABLE ... about THE NINTH CENTURY, IT APPEARS AS IF ALL THE CHAZARS WERE JEWS AND THAT THEY HAD BEEN CONVERTED TO JUDAISM ONLY A SHORT TIME BEFORE... It was one of the successors of Bulan named Obadiah, who regenerated the kingdom and STRENGTHENED THE JEWISH RELIGION. He invited Jewish scholars to settle in his dominions, and founded SYNAGOGUES AND SCHOOLS. The people were instructed in the Bible, Mishnah, and the TALMUD and in the `divine service of the hazzanim'.. In their writings the CHAZARS USED THE HEBREW LETTERS ... THE CHAZAR LANGUAGES PREDOMINATED... Obadiah was succeeded by his son Isaac; Isaac by his son Moses (or Manasseh II); the latter by his son Nisi; and Nisi by his son Aaron II.

King Joseph himself was a son of Aaron, AND ASCENDED THE

THRONE IN ACCORDANCE WITH THE LAW OF THE CHAZARS RELATING TO SUCCESSION ... The king had twenty-five wives, all of royal blood, and sixty concubines, all famous beauties. Each one slept in a separate tent and was watched by a eunuch ... THIS SEEMS TO HAVE BEEN THE BEGINNING OF THE DOWNFALL OF THE CHAZAR KINGDOM ... The Russian Varangians established themselves at Kiev... until the final conquest of the Chazars by the Russians ... After a hard fight the Russians conquered the Chazars... Four years later the Russians conquered all the Chazarian territory east of the Azov ... many members of the Chazarian royal family emigrated to Spain... Some went to Hungary, BUT THE GREAT MASS OF THE PEOPLE REMAINED IN THEIR NATIVE COUNTRY."

The greatest historian on the origin and the history of the so-called or self-styled "Jews" in Eastern Europe was Professor H. Graetz, himself a so-called or self-styled "Jew". Professor H. Graetz points out in his famous "History of the Jews" that when so-called or self-styled "Jews" in other countries heard a rumor about so-called or self-styled "Jews" in the Khazar Kingdom they believed these converted Khazars to be the "lost ten tribes". These rumors were no doubt responsible for the legend which grew up that Palestine was the "homeland" of the converted Khazars. On page 141 in his "History of the Jews" Professor H. Graetz states:

"The Chazars professed a coarse religion, which was combined with sensuality and lewdness...After Obadia came a long series of Jewish Chagans (kings), for ACCORDING TO A FUNDAMENTAL LAW OF THE STATE ONLY JEWISH RULERS WERE PERMITTED TO ASCEND THE THRONE...For some time THE JEWS OF OTHER COUNTRIES HAD NO KNOWLEDGE OF THE CONVERSION OF THIS POWERFUL KINGDOM TO JUDAISM, and when at last a vague rumor to this effect reached them, THEY WERE OF THE OPINION THAT CHAZARIA WAS PEOPLED BY THE REMNANT OF THE FORMER TEN TRIBES."

When the Khazars in the 1st century B.C. invaded eastern Europe their mother-tongue was an Asiatic language, referred to in the Jewish Encyclopedia as the "Khazar languages". They were primitive Asiatic dialects without any alphabet or any written form. When King Bulan was converted in the 7th century he decreed that the Hebrew characters he saw in the Talmud and other Hebrew documents was thereupon to become the alphabet for the Khazar language. The Hebrew characters were adopted to the phonetics of the spoken Khazar language. The Khazars adopted the characters of the so-called Hebrew language in order to provide a means for providing a written record of their speech. The adoption of the Hebrew characters had no racial, political or religious implication.

The western European uncivilized nations which had no alphabet for their spoken language adopted the alphabet of the Latin language under comparable circumstances. With the invasion of Western Europe by the Romans the civilization and the culture of the Romans was introduced into these uncivilized areas. Thus the Latin alphabet was adopted for the language of the French, Spanish, ENGLISH, Swedish and many other western European languages. These languages were completely foreign to each other yet they all used the same alphabet. The Romans brought their alphabet with their culture to these uncivilized nations exactly like the rabbis brought the Hebrew alphabet from Babylonia to the Khazars when they introduced writing to them in the form of the Talmud's alphabet.

Since the conquest of the Khazars by the Russians and the disappearance of the Khazar Kingdom the language of the Khazars is known as Yiddish for about six centuries the so-called or self- styled "Jews" of eastern Europe have referred to themselves while still resident in their native eastern European countries as "Yiddish" by nationality. They identified themselves as "Yiddish" rather than as Russian, Polish, Galician, Lithuanian, Rumanian, Hungarian or by the nation of which they were citizens. They also referred to the common language they all spoke as "Yiddish" also. There are today in New York City as you know, my dear Dr. Goldstein, many "Yiddish" newspapers, "Yiddish" theaters, and many other cultural organizations of so-called or self-styled "Jews" from eastern Europe which are identified publicly by the word "Yiddish" in their title.

Before it became known as the "Yiddish" language, the mother-tongue of the Khazars added many words to its limited ancient vocabulary as necessity required. These words were acquired from the languages of its neighboring nations with whom they had political, social or economic relations.

Languages of all nations add to their vocabularies in the same way. The Khazars adapted words to their requirements form the German, the Slavonic and the Baltic languages. The Khazars adopted a great number of words from the German language. The Germans had a much more advanced civilization than their Khazar neighbors and the Khazars sent their children to German schools and universities.

The "Yiddish" language is not a German dialect. Many people are led to believe so because "Yiddish" has borrowed so many words from the German language. If "Yiddish" is a German dialect acquired from the Germans then what language did the Khazars speak for 1000 years they existed in Eastern Europe before they acquired culture from the Germans? The Khazars must have spoken some language when they invaded Eastern Europe. What was that language? When did they discard it? How did the entire Khazar population discard one language and adopt another all of a sudden? The idea is too absurd to discuss. "Yiddish" is the modern name for the ancient mother-tongue of the Khazars with added German, Slavonic and Baltic adopted and adapted numerous words.

"Yiddish" must not be confused with "Hebrew" because they both use the same characters as their alphabets. There is not one word of "Yiddish" in ancient "Hebrew" nor is there one word of ancient "Hebrew" in "Yiddish". As I stated before, they are as totally different as Swedish and Spanish which both likewise use the same Latin characters for their alphabets. The "Yiddish" languages is the cultural common denominator for all the so-called or self-styled "Jews" in or from eastern Europe. To the so-called or self-styled "Jews" in and from Eastern Europe, "Yiddish" serves them like the English language serves the populations of the 48 states of the United States. Their cultural common denominator throughout the 48 states is the English language, or wherever they may emigrate and resettle. The English language is the tie which binds them to each other. It is the same with the "Yiddish" language and so-called or self-styled "Jews" throughout the world.

"Yiddish" serves another very useful purpose for so-called or self-styled "Jews" throughout the world. They possess in "Yiddish" what no other national, racial or religious group can claim. Approximately 90% of the world's so-called or self-styled "Jews" living in 42 countries of the world today are either emigrants from eastern Europe, or their parents emigrated from eastern Europe. "Yiddish" is a language common to all of them as their first or second language according to where they were born. It is an "international" language to them. Regardless of what country in the world they may settle in they will always find co-religionists who also speak "Yiddish". "Yiddish" enjoys other international advantages too obvious to describe here. "Yiddish" is the modern language of a nation which has lost its existence as a nation. "Yiddish" never had a religious implication, although using Hebrew characters for its alphabet. It must not be confused with words like "Jewish". But it is very much.

Directly north of the Khazar Kingdom at the height of its power a small Slavic state was organized in 820 A.D. on the south shore of the Gulf of Finland where it flows into the Baltic Sea. This small state was organized by a small group of Varangians from the Scandinavian peninsula on the opposite shore of the Baltic Sea. The native population of this newly formed state consisted of nomad Slavs who had made their home in this area from earliest recorded history. This infant nation was even small than our state of Delaware. This newly-born state however was the embryo which developed into the great Russian Empire. In less than 1000 years since 820 A.D. this synthetic nation expanded its borders by ceaseless conquests until it now includes more than

9,500,000 square miles in Europe and Asia, or more than three times the area of continental United States, and they have not stopped.

During the 10th, 11th, 12th, and 13th centuries the rapidly expanding Russian nation gradually swallowed up the Khazar kingdom, its neighbor directly to the south. The conquest of the Khazar Kingdom by the Russians supplies history with the explanation for the presence after the 13th century of the large number of so-called or self-styled "Jews" in Russia. The large number of so-called or self-styled "Jews" in Russia and in Eastern Europe after the destruction of the Khazar Kingdom were thereafter no longer known as Khazars but as the "Yiddish" populations of these many countries. They so refer to themselves today.

In the many wars with her neighbors in Europe after the 13th century Russia was required to cede to her victors large areas which were originally part of the Khazar Kingdom. In this manner Poland, Lithuania, Galicia, Hungary, Rumania, and Austria acquired from Russia territory originally a part of the Khazar Kingdom. Together with this territory these nations acquired a segment of the population of so-called or self-styled "Jews" descended from the Khazars who once occupied the territory. These frequent boundary changes by the nations in eastern Europe explains the presence today of so-called or self-styled "Jews" in all these countries who all trace their ancestry back to the converted Khazars. Their common language, their common culture, their common religion, and their common racial characteristics classify them all beyond any question of doubt with the Khazars who invaded Eastern Europe in the 1st century B.C. and were converted to "Talmudism" in the 7th century.

The so-called or self-styled "Jews" throughout the world today of eastern European origin make up at least 90% of the world's total present population of so-called or self-styled "Jews". The conversion of King Bulan and the Khazar nation in the 7th century accomplished for "Talmudism", or for "Judaism" as "Talmudism" is called today, what the conversion of Constantine and the western European nations accomplished for Christianity. Christianity was a small comparatively unimportant religious belief practiced principally in the eastern Mediterranean area until the conversion to the Christian faith of the large populations of the western European pagan nations after the conversion of Constantine. "Talmudism", or "Judaism" as "Talmudism" is known today, was given its greatest stimulus in all its history with the conversion of the large pagan Khazar population in the 7th century. Without the conversion of the Khazar population it is doubtful if "Talmudism", or "Judaism" as "Talmudism" is known today, could have survived. "Talmudism", the civil and religious code of the Pharisees, most likely would have passed out of existence like the many other creeds and cults practiced by the peoples in that area before, during and after "Pharisaism" assumed its prominent position among these creeds and cults in the time of Jesus. "Talmudism", as "Pharisaism" was called later, would have disappeared with all its contemporary creeds and cults but for the conversion of the Khazars to "Talmudism" in the 7th century. At that time "Talmudism" was well on its way towards complete oblivion.

In the year 986 A.D. the ruler of Russia, Vladimir III, became a convert to the Christian faith in order to marry a Catholic Slavonic princess of a neighboring sovereign state. The marriage was otherwise impossible. Vladimir III thereupon also made his newly-acquired Christian faith the state religion of Russia replacing the pagan worship formerly practiced in Russia since it was founded in 820 A.D. Vladimir III and his successors as the rulers of Russia attempted in vain to convert his so-called or self-styled "Jews", now Russian subjects, to Russia's Christian state religion and to adopt the customs and culture of the numerically predominant Russian Christian population. The so-called or self- styled "Jews" in Russia refused and resisted this plan vigorously. They refused to adopt the Russian alphabet in place of the Hebrew characters used in writing their "Yiddish" language. They resisted the substitution of the Russian language for "Yiddish" as their mother-tongue. They opposed every attempt to bring about the complete assimilation of the former sovereign Khazar nation into the Russian nation. They resisted with every means at their disposal. The many forms of tension which resulted produced situations described by history as "massacres", "pogroms", "persecution", discrimination, etc.

In Russia at that period of history it was the custom as in other Christian countries in Europe at that time to take an oath, vow or pledge of loyalty to the rulers, the nobles, the feudal landholders and others in the name of Jesus Christ. It was after the conquest of the Khazars by the Russians that the wording of the "Kol Nidre" (All Vows) prayer was altered. The new altered version of the "Kol Nidre" (All Vows) prayer is referred to in the Talmud as "the law of revocation in advance". The "Kol Nidre" (All Vows) prayer was regarded as a "law". The effect of this "LAW OF REVOCATION IN ADVANCE" obtained for all who recited it each year on the eve of the Day of Atonement divine dispensation from all obligations acquired under "oaths, vows and pledges" to be made or taken in the COMING YEAR. The recital of the "Kol Nidre" (All Vows) prayer on the eve of the Day of Atonement released those so-called or self-styled "Jews" from any obligation under "oaths, vows or pledges" entered into during the NEXT TWELVE MONTHS. The "oaths, vows and pledges" made or taken by so-called or self-styled "Jews" were made or taken "with tongue in cheek" for twelve months.

The altered version of the "Kol Nidre" (All Vows) prayer created serious difficulties for the so-called or self-styled "Jews" when its wording became public property. It apparently did not remain a secret very long, although the Talmud states "the law of revocation in advance was not made public". The altered version of the "Kol Nidre" (All Vows) prayer soon became known as the "Jews Vow" and cast serious doubt upon "oaths, vows or pledges" given to Christians by so-called or self-styled "Jews". Christians soon believed that "oaths, vows or pledges" were quite worthless when given by so-called or self-styled "Jews". This was the basis for so-called "discrimination" by governments, nobles, feudal landholders, and others who required oaths of allegiance and loyalty from those who entered their service.

An intelligent attempt was made to correct this situation by a group of German rabbis in 1844. In that year they called an international conference of rabbis in Brunswick, Germany. They attempted to have the "Kol Nidre" (All Vows) prayer completely eliminated from the Day of Atonement ceremonies, and entirely abolish from any religious service of their faith. They felt that this secular prologue to the Day of Atonement ceremonies was void of any spiritual implication and did not belong in any synagogue ritual. However the preponderant majority of the rabbis attending that conference in Brunswick came from eastern Europe. They represented congregations of Yiddish-speaking so-called or self- styled "Jews" of converted Khazar origin in Eastern Europe. They insisted that the altered version of the "Kol Nidre" (All Vows) prayer be retained exactly as it was then recited on the Day of Atonement. They demanded that it be allowed to remain as it had been recited in Eastern Europe since the change by Meir ben Samuel six centuries earlier. It is today recited in exactly that form throughout the world by so-called or self-styled "Jews". Will the 150,000,000 Christians in the United States react any differently when they become more aware of its insidious implications?

How genuine can the implications, inferences and innuendoes of the so-called "brotherhood" and "interfaith" movements be under these circumstances? These so-called movements are sweeping the nations like prairie fires. If the Talmud is the axis of the political, economic, cultural and social attitudes and activities of so-called or self-styled "Jews" participating in these two so-called movements, how genuine are the "oaths, vows or pledges" taken or given in connection with these two so-called movements by so-called or self-styled "Jews"? It would be a superlative gesture of "brotherhood" or of "interfaith" if the National Conference of Christians and Jews succeeded in expunging from the Talmud all anti-Christ, anti-Christian, and anti- Christianity passages. At a cost of many millions of dollars the National Conference of Christians and Jews succeeded in expunging from the New Testament passages which so-called or self-styled "Jews" regarded as offensive to their faith. A great portion of the cost was supplied by so-called or self-styled "Jews". Christians might now supply funds to expunge from the Talmud passages offensive to the Christian faith. Otherwise the so-called "brotherhood" and "interfaith" movements are merely mockeries.

The National Conference of Christians and Jews might look into the millions of dollars being invested today by so-called or self-styled "Jews" to insure that the Talmud shall remain the axis of political, economic, cultural and social attitudes and activities of so- called or self-styled "Jews" today, and future generations. Violating the basic principle of "brotherhood" and "interfaith" so-called or self-styled "Jews" are spending millions of dollars each year to establish and equip quarters where the teachings of the Talmud can be indoctrinated into the minds of children from the time they are able to read and write. These few news items were selected from hundreds like them which are appearing daily in newspapers clear across the nation:

"Two new Jewish Centers, built at a cost of $300,000 will be opened to 1000 students for daily and Sunday school activities next month, it was announced by the Associated Talmud Torahs."

(*Chicago Herald-Tribune*, 8/19/50)


"The Yeshiva School Department now provides daytime an approved English-Hebrew curriculum for grades 1 to 5 (aged 5½ to 10). The afternoon Talmud Torah has opened a new beginner's class and is accepting enrollment of advanced as well as beginner students."

(*Jewish Voice*, 9/18/53)


"RABBI TO TALK ON TALMUD TO SHOLEM MEN. Dr. David Graubert presiding rabbi of Bet Din, and professor of rabbinical literature at the College of Jewish Studies, will present the first of his series of four lectures, ``The World of the Talmud'.

(*Chicago Tribune*, 10/29/53)


"MARYLAND GRANTS DEGREE IN TALMUD. Baltimore, (JTA). New Israel Rabbinical College has been granted here authority by the Maryland State Board of Education to issue degrees of Master of Talmudic Law and Doctor of Talmudic Law."

(*Jewish Voice*, 1/9/53)


"TALMUD LESSONS ON AIR FROM JERUSALEM. Weekly radio lectures on the Talmud, in English, will be available shortly on tape recordings for local stations in the United States and Canada, it was announced today."

(*California Jewish Voice*, 1/11/52)

Earlier in this letter, my dear Dr. Goldstein, you remember reading a quotation by the most eminent authority on the Talmud to the effect that "THE MODERN JEW IS A PRODUCT OF THE TALMUD." Would it surprise you to learn that many Christians also are the "PRODUCT OF THE TALMUD". The teachings of the Talmud are accepted by Christians in the highest echelons. I will only quote one of the subject of the Talmud, the former President of the United States. In 1951 President Truman was presented with his second set of the "63 books" of the Talmud. On the occasion of his acceptance the newspapers carried the following news item:

"Mr. Truman thanked us for the books and said that he was glad to get them as `I have read many more of the ones presented four years ago than a lot of people think'. He said that he did read a lot and that the book he read the most is the Talmud which contains much sound reasoning and good philosophy of life".

Former President Truman says he benefits by "much sound reasoning" and his brand of "good philosophy of life" which absorbs from the "book that he reads the most." His recent term in office reflected his study of the Talmud. No one familiar with the Talmud will deny that. But does our former President Truman known that Jesus did not feel the way he feels about the Talmud? The "much good reasoning" and the "good philosophy of life" in the Talmud were constantly and consistently denounced by Jesus in no uncertain terms. Former President Truman should refresh his memory by reading the New Testament passages where Jesus expresses Himself on the question of the Pharisees and their Talmud. Will Mr. Truman state that in his opinion the Talmud was the "sort of book" from which Jesus "drew the teachings which enabled him to revolutionize the world" on "moral and religious subjects"?

Before leaving the Talmud as my subject I would like to refer to the most authentic analysis of the Talmud which has ever been written. You should obtain a copy of it and read it. You will be amply rewarded for your trouble in finding a copy of it. I can doubly assure you. The name of the book is "The Talmud". It was written almost a century ago in French by Arsene Darmesteter. In 1897 it was translated into English by the celebrated Henrietta Szold and published by the Jewish Publication Society of America in Philadelphia. Henrietta Szold was an outstanding educator and Zionist and one of the most notable and admirable so-called or self- styled "Jews" of this century. Henrietta Szold's translation of Arsene Darmesteter's "The Talmud" is a classic. You will never understand the Talmud until you have read it. I will quote from it sparingly:

"Now Judaism finds its expression in the Talmud, which is not a remote suggestion and a faint echo thereof, but in which it has become incarnate, in which it has taken form, passing from a state of abstraction into the domain of real things. THE STUDY OF JUDAISM IS THAT OF THE TALMUD, AS THE STUDY OF THE TALMUD IS THAT OF JUDAISM . . . THEY ARE TWO INSEPARABLE THINGS, OR BETTER, THEY ARE ONE AND THE SAME . . . Accordingly, the Talmud is the completest expression of religious movement, and this code of endless prescriptions and minute ceremonials represents in its perfection the total work of the religious idea . . . The miracle was accomplished by a book, the Talmud . . . The Talmud, in turn, is composed of two distinct parts, the Mishna and the Gemara; the former the text, the latter the commentary upon the text . . . By the term Mishna we designate A COLLECTION OF DECISIONS AND TRADITIONAL LAWS, EMBRACING ALL DEPARTMENTS OF LEGISLATION, CIVIL AND RELIGIOUS . . . This code, which was the work of several generations of Rabbis . . . Nothing, indeed can EQUAL THE IMPORTANCE OF THE TALMUD unless it be the ignorance that prevails concerning it . . . This explains how it happens that a single page of the Talmud contains three or four different languages, or rather specimens of one language at three or four stages of degeneracy . . . Many a Mischna of five or six lines is accompanied by fifty or sixty pages of explanation . . . is Law in all its authority; it constitutes dogma and cult; it is the fundamental element of the Talmud . . . The DAILY STUDY OF THE TALMUD, WHICH AMONG JEWS BEGAN WITH THE AGE OF TEN TO END LIFE ITSELF, necessarily was a severe gymnastic for the mind, thanks to which IT ACQUIRED INCOMPARABLE SUBTLETY AND ACUMEN . . . SINCE IT ASPIRES TO ONE THING: TO ESTABLISH FOR JUDAISM A 'CORPUS JURIS ECCLESIASTICI.'"

The above quotations were culled from a treatise intended to sugar-coat the Talmud. In painting a nice word-picture of the Talmud the author could not escape mentioning the above facts also. Coming from this source under the circumstances the facts stated above do not add glory to the Talmud.

"The Talmud Unmasked, The Secret Rabbinical Teachings Concerning Christians," was written by Rev. I. B. Pranaitis, Master of Theology and Professor of the Hebrew Language at the Imperial Ecclesiastical Academy of the Roman Catholic Church in Old St. Petersburg, Russia. The Rev. Pranaitis was the greatest of the students of the Talmud. His complete command of the Hebrew language qualified him to analyze the Talmud as few men in history.

The Rev. Pranaitis scrutinized the Talmud for passages referring to Jesus,

Christians and the Christian faith. These passages were translated by him into Latin. Hebrew lends itself to translation into Latin better than it does directly into English. The translation of the passages of the Talmud referring to Jesus, Christians and Christian faith were printed in Latin by the Imperial Academy of Sciences in St. Petersburg in 1893 with the Imprimatur of his Archbishop. The translation from the Latin into English was made by great Latin scholars in the United States in 1939 with funds provided by wealthy Americans for that purpose.

In order not to leave any loose ends on the subject of the Talmud's reference to Jesus, to Christians and to the Christian faith I will below summarize translations into English from the Latin texts of Rev. Pranaitis' "The Talmud Unmasked, The Secret Rabbinical Teachings Concerning Christians". It would require too much space to quote these passages verbatim with their footnotes form the Soncino Edition in English.

First I will summarize the references by Rev. Pranaitis referring to Jesus in the Talmud in the original texts translated by him into Latin, and from Latin into English:

Sanhedrin, 67a -- Jesus referred to as the son of Pandira, a soldier.

Kallah, 1b. (18b) -- Illegitimate and conceived during menstruation.

Sanhedrin, 67a -- Hanged on the eve of Passover.

Toldath Jeschu -- Birth related in most shameful expressions

Abhodah Zarah II -- Referred to as the son of Pandira, a Roman soldier.

Schabbath XIV -- Again referred to as the son of Pandira, the Roman.

Sanhedrin, 43a -- On the eve of Passover they hanged Jesus.

Schabbath, 104b -- Called a fool and no one pays attention to fools.

Toldoth Jeschu -- Judas and Jesus engaged in quarrel with filth.

Sanhedrin, 103a. -- Suggested corrupts his morals and dishonors self.

Sanhedrin, 107b. -- Seduced, corrupted and destroyed Israel.

Zohar III, (282) -- Died like a beast and buried in animal's dirt heap.

Hilkoth Melakhim -- Attempted to prove Christians err in worship of Jesus

Abhodah Zarah, 21a -- Reference to worship of Jesus in homes unwanted.

Orach Chaiim, 113 -- Avoid appearance of paying respect to Jesus.

Iore dea, 150, 2 -- Do not appear to pay respect to Jesus by accident.

Abhodah Zarah (6a) -- False teachings to worship on first day of Sabbath

The above are a few selected from a very complicated arrangement in which many references are obscured by intricate reasoning. The following are a few summarized references to Christians and the Christian faith although not always expressed in exactly that manner. There are eleven names used in the Talmud for non-Talmud followers, by which Christians are meant. Besides Nostrim, from Jesus the Nazarene, Christians are called by all the names used in the Talmud to designate all non-"Jews": Minim, Edom, Abhodan Zarah, Akum. Obhde Elilim, Nokrim, Amme Haarets, Kuthim, Apikorosim, and Goim. Besides supplying the names by which Christians are called in the Talmud, the passages quoted below indicate what kind of people the Talmud pictures the Christians to be, and what the Talmud says about the religious worship of Christians:

Hilkhoth Maakhaloth -- Christians are idolaters, must not associate.

Abhodah Zarah (22a) -- Do not associate with gentiles, they shed blood.

Iore Dea (153, 2) -- Must not associate with Christians, shed blood.

Abhodah Zarah (25b) -- Beware of Christians when walking abroad with them.

Orach Chaiim (20, 2) -- Christians disguise themselves to kill Jews.

Abhodah Zarah (15b) -- Suggest Christians have sex relations with animals.

Abhodah Zarah (22a) -- Suspect Christians of intercourse with animals.

Schabbath (145b) -- Christians unclean because they eat accordingly

Abhodah Zarah (22b) -- Christians unclean because they not at Mount Sinai.

Iore Dea (198, 48) -- Clean female Jews contaminated meeting Christians.

Kerithuth (6b p. 78) -- Jews called men, Christians not called men.

Makkoth (7b) -- Innocent of murder if intent was to kill Christian.

Orach Chaiim(225, 10) -- Christians and animals grouped for comparisons.

Midrasch Talpioth 225 -- Christians created to minister to Jews always.

Orach Chaiim 57, 6a -- Christians to be pitied more than sick pigs.

Zohar II (64b) -- Christian idolaters likened to cows and asses.

Kethuboth (110b) -- Psalmist compares Christians to unclean beasts.

Sanhedrin (74b). Tos. -- Sexual intercourse of Christian like that of beast.

Kethuboth (3b) -- The seed of Christian is valued as seed of beast.

Kidduschim (68a) -- Christians like the people of an ass.

Eben Haezar (44,8) -- Marriages between Christian and Jews null.

Zohar (II, 64b) -- Christian birth rate must be diminished materially.

Zohar (I, 28b) -- Christian idolaters children of Eve's serpent.

Zohar (I, 131a) -- Idolatrous people (Christians) befoul the world.

Emek Haschanach(17a) -- Non-Jews' souls come from death and death's shadow.

Zohar (I, 46b, 47a) -- Souls of gentiles have unclean divine origins.

Rosch Haschanach(17a) -- Non-Jews souls go down to hell.

Iore Dea (337, 1) -- Replace dead Christians like lost cow or ass.

Iebhammoth (61a) -- Jews called men, but not Christians called men.

Abhodah Zarah (14b) T -- Forbidden to sell religious works to Christians

Abhodah Zarah (78) -- Christian churches are places of idolatry.

Iore Dea (142, 10) -- Must keep far away physically from churches.

Iore Dea (142, 15) -- Must not listen to church music or look at idols

Iore Dea (143, 1) -- Must not rebuild homes destroyed near churches.

Hilkoth Abh. Zar (10b) -- Jews must not resell broken chalices to Christians.

Chullin (91b) -- Jews possess dignity even an angel cannot share.

Sanhedrin, 58b -- To strike Israelite like slapping face of God.

Chagigah, 15b -- A Jew considered good in spite of sins he commits.

Gittin (62a) -- Jew stay away from Christian homes on holidays.

Choschen Ham. (26, 1) -- Jew must not sue before a Christian judge or laws.

Choschen Ham (34, 19) -- Christian or servant cannot become  witnesses.

Iore Dea (112, 1) -- Avoid eating with Christians, breeds familiarity.

Abhodah Zarah (35b) -- Do not drink milk from a cow milked by Christian.

Iore dea (178, 1) -- Never imitate customs of Christians, even hair-comb.

Abhodah Zarah (72b) -- Wine touched by Christians must be thrown away.

Iore Dea (120, 1) -- Bought-dishes from Christians must be thrown away.

Abhodah Zarah (2a) -- For three days before Christian festivals, avoid all.

Abhodah Zarah (78c) -- Festivals of followers of Jesus regarded as idolatry.

Iore Dea (139, 1) -- Avoid things used by Christians in their worship.

Abhodah Zarah (14b) -- Forbidden to sell Christians articles for worship.

Iore Dea (151, 1) H. -- Do not sell water to Christians articles for baptisms.

Abhodah Zarah (2a, 1) -- Do not trade with Christians on their feast days.

Abhodah Zarah (1, 2) -- Now permitted to trade with Christians on such days.

Abhodah Zarah (2aT) -- Trade with Christians because they have money to pay.

Iore Dea (148, 5) -- If Christian is not devout, may send him gifts.

Hilkoth Akum (IX, 2) -- Send gifts to Christians only if they are irreligious.

Iore Dea (81, 7 Ha) -- Christian wet-nurses to be avoided because dangerous.

Iore Dea (153, 1 H) -- Christian nurse will lead children to heresy.

Iore Dea (155, 1) -- Avoid Christian doctors not well known to neighbors.

Peaschim (25a) -- Avoid medical help from idolaters, Christians meant.

Iore Dea (156, 1) -- Avoid Christian barbers unless escorted by Jews.

Abhodah Zarah (26a) -- Avoid Christian midwives dangerous when alone.

Hilkoth Akum (X, 6) -- Help needy Christians if it will promote peace.

Iore Dea (148, 12H) -- Hide hatred for Christians at their celebrations.

Abhodah Zarah (20a) -- Never praise Christians lest it be believed true.

Iore Dea (151, 14) -- Not allowed to praise Christians to add to glory.

Hilkoth Akum (V, 12) -- Quote Scriptures to forbid mention of Christian god.

Iore Dea (146, 15) -- Refer to Christian religious articles with contempt.

Iore Dea (147, 5) -- Deride Christian religious articles without wishes.

Hilkoth Akum (X, 5) -- No gifts to Christians, gifts to converts.

Iore Dea (151, 11) -- Gifts forbidden to Christians, encourages friendship.

Iore Dea (335, 43) -- Exile for that Jew who sells farm to Christian.

Iore Dea (154, 2) -- Forbidden to teach a trade to a Christian

Babha Bathra (54b) -- Christian property belongs to first person claiming.

Choschen Ham (183, 7) -- Keep what Christian overpays in error.

Choschen Ham (226, 1) -- Jew may keep lost property of Christian found by Jew.

Babha Kama (113b) -- It is permitted to deceive Christians.

Choschen Ham (183, 7) -- Jews must divide what they overcharge Christians.

Choschen Ham (156, 5) -- Jews must not take Christian customers from Jews.

Iore Dea (157,2) H -- May deceive Christians that believe Christian tenets.

Abhodah Zarah (54a) --Usury may be practiced upon Christians or apostates.

Iore Dea (159, 1) -- Usury permitted now for any reason to Christians

Babha Kama (113a) -- Jew may lie and perjure to condemn a Christian

Babha Kama (113b) -- Name of God not profaned when lying to Christians.

Kallah (1b, p.18) -- Jew may perjure himself with a clear conscience.

Schabbouth Hag (6d) -- Jews may swear falsely by use of subterfuge wording.

Zohar (1,160a) -- Jews must always try to deceive Christians.

Iore Dea (158, 1) -- Do not cure Christians unless it makes enemies.

Orach Cahiim (330, 2) -- Do not assist Christian's childbirth on Saturday.

Choschen Ham (425, 5) -- Unless believes in Torah do not prevent his death.

Iore Dea (158, 1) -- Christians not enemies must not be saved either.

Hilkkoth Akum (X, 1) -- Do not save Christians in danger of death.

Choschen Ham (386, 10) -- A spy may be killed even before he confesses.

Abhodah Zorah (26b) -- Apostates to be thrown into well, not rescued.

Choschen Ham(388, 15) -- Kill those who give Israelites' money to Christians

Sanhedrin (59a) -- `Prying into Jews' "Law" to get death penalty

Hilkhoth Akum (X, 2) -- Baptized Jews are to be put to death

Iore Dea (158, 2) Hag -- Kill renegades who turn to Christian rituals.

Choschen Ham (425, 5) -- Those who do not believe in Torah are to be killed.

Hilkhoth tesch.III, 8 -- Christians and others deny the "Law" of the Torah.

Zohar (I,25a) -- Christians are to be destroyed as idolaters.

Zohar (II,19a) -- Captivity of Jews end when Christian princes die.

Zohar (I,219b) -- Princes of Christians are idolaters, must die.

Obadiam -- When Rome is destroyed, Israel will be redeemed.

Abhodah Zarah (26b) T. -- "Even the best of the Goim should be killed."

Sepher Or Israel 177b -- If Jew kills Christian commits no sin.

Ialkut Simoni (245c) -- Shedding blood of impious offers sacrifice to God.

Zohar (II, 43a) -- Extermination of Christians necessary sacrifice.

Zohar (L, 28b, 39a) -- High place in heaven for those who kill idolaters.

Hilkhoth Akum (X, 1) -- Make no agreements and show no mercy to Christians

Hilkhoth Akum (X, 1) -- Either turn them away from their idols or kill.

Hilkhoth Akum (X, 7) -- Allow no idolaters to remain where Jews are strong.

Choschen Ham (388, 16) -- All contribute to expense of killing traitor.

Pesachim (49b) -- No need of prayers while beheading on Sabbath.

Schabbath (118a) -- Prayers to save from punishment of coming Messiah.


In the Library of Congress and the New York Public Library, unless recently removed, you can find a copy of "The Talmud Unmasked, The Secret Rabbinical Teachings Concerning Christians" by the Rev. I. B. Pranaitis. A copy of the original work printed in St. Petersburg, Russia in 1892 can be made available to you by our mutual friend if you are interested in reading the above passages in the original Hebrew text with their Latin translation. I trust my summaries correctly explain the original text. I believe they do. If I am in error in any way please be so kind as to let me know. It was very difficult to reduce them to short summaries.

The National Conference of Christians and Jews need not scrutinize the "63 books" of the Talmud to discover all the anti-Christ, anti-Christian, and anti-Christian faith passages in the books which are "THE LEGAL CODE WHICH FORMS THE BASIS OF JEWISH RELIGIOUS LAW" and which is "THE TEXTBOOK USED IN THE TRAINING OF RABBIS". They can also keep that, as Rabbi Morris Kertzer also points out, as explained earlier, that "ADULTS STUDY ANCIENT WRITINGS TOO... IN... GROUP DISCUSSION OF TALMUD BEFORE EVENING PRAYER". If the National Conference of Christians and Jews are genuinely interested in "interfaith" and "brotherhood" do you not think, my dear Dr. Goldstein, that they should compel a start at once to expunge from the Talmud the anti-Christ, anti-Christian, and anti-Christianity passages from the Talmud in the "brotherly" way they expunged passages from the New Testament? Will you ask them?

Throughout the world the Oxford English Dictionary is accepted as the most authoritative and authentic source for information on the origin, definition and use of words in the English language. Authorities in all fields everywhere accept the Oxford English Dictionary brings out clearly that "Judaist" and "Judaic" are the correct forms for the improper and incorrect misused and misleading "Jews" and "Jewish". You will agree completely with the Oxford English Dictionary if you consider the matter carefully. "Judaist" and "Judaic" are correct. "Jews" and "Jewish" are incorrect. "Jew" and "Jewish" do not belong in the English language if the use of the correct words is of interest to the English-speaking peoples.

The so-called or self-styled "Jews" cannot truthfully describe themselves as "Jews" because they are not in any sense "Judeans". They can correctly identify themselves by their religious belief if they so wish by identifying themselves as "Judaists". A "Judaist" is a person who professes so-called "Judaism" as his religious belief, according to the Oxford English Dictionary. The origin of "Jew" has not its roots in "Judaism" as explained. The adjective form of "Judaist" is "Judaic". "Jewish" as an adjective is just as incorrect as "Jew" is as a noun. "Jewish" has no reason to exist.

Well-planned and well-financed publicity by so-called or self-styled "Jews" in English-speaking countries in the 18th, 19th, and 20th centuries created a wide acceptance and use for "Jewish". "Jewish" is being used today in many ways that are no less fantastic and grotesque than incorrect and inaccurate. "Jewish" is used today to describe everything from "Jewish blood", whatever that may be, to "Jewish Rye Bread", strange as that may sound. The many implications, inferences and innuendoes of "Jewish" today resulting from its commercial uses beggar description.

At the 1954 annual meeting of the St. Paul Guild in the Plaza Hotel in New York City before more than 1000 Catholics, a Roman Catholic priest who was the main speaker and the guest of honor referred to "my Jewish blood". It just happens that this priest was born a so-called or self-styled "Jews" in eastern Europe and was converted to Catholicism there about 25 years ago. It seems unique that a priest who has professed Catholicism that length of time should mention "my Jewish blood" to Catholics. The radio blasts and the outdoor signs blazon "Levy's Jewish Rye Bread", in the same city at the same time. Between these two extremes are countless other products and other services which advertise themselves in print, on radio and television, as "Jewish".

This priest who talks to Catholics about "my Jewish blood" when he addresses audiences also refers to the "Jewish blood" of Mary, Holy Mother of Jesus, to the "Jewish blood" of the Apostles, and to the "Jewish blood" of the early Christians. What he means by "my Jewish blood" mystifies those Catholics who hear him. They query "What is `Jewish blood' "? They ask what happens to "Jewish blood" when so-called or self-styled "Jews" are converted to Catholicism? And in the extreme case when a so-called or self- styled "Jew" becomes a Roman Catholic priest? How is "Jewish blood" biologically different from the blood of persons who profess other religious faiths, they ask. It is hard for me to believe that there is anything biologically different which determines characteristics typical of a specific religious belief. Are the inherent racial and national characteristics determined by religious dogma or doctrine?

The word "Jewess" raises a similar question. If "Jewess" is the female for the male "Jew" I must admit that I have been unable to find female as well as male designation for persons professing any religious belief other than so-called "Judaism". Are there any other that you know? I have searched for the female of Catholicism, Protestantism, Hindu, Moslem, and others but without success. It seems very popular now to refer to Mary, Holy Mother of Jesus, as a "Jewess". It does seem unrealistic to identify the sex of members of any religious belief by appropriate designations. If the word "Jew" is regarded as descriptive of a race or a nation, as is often the case, it is equally unrealistic to indicate the sex of members of a race or a nation by a suffix used for that purpose. I know of no case in that respect except "Negress", and the Negro race strongly objects to the use of that designation, and strongly.

Another word is creating more problems among Christians. I refer to "Judeo-Christian". You see it more and more day by day. Based on our present knowledge of history, and on good sense applied to theology, the term "Judea-Christian" presents a strange combination. Does "Judeo" refer to ancient "Pharisaism", or to "Talmudism", or to so-called "Judaism"? In view of what we know today, how can there be "Judeo-Christian" anything? Based upon what is now known "Judeo-Christian" is as unrealistic as it would be to say anything is "hot-cold" , or "old-young", or "heavy-light", or that a person was "healthy-sick", or "poor-rich", or "dumb-smart", or "ignorant-educated", or "happy-sad". These words are antonyms, not synonyms. "Judeo-Christian" in the light of incontestable facts are also antonyms, not synonyms as so-called or self-styled "Jews" would like Christians to believe. More sand for Christian's eyes.

An "Institute of Judeo-Christian Studies" has been established by Seton Hall University. It is actually a "one-man Institute". Father John M. Oesterreicher is the "one-man Institute". The "Institute of Judaeo-Christian Studies" occupies a small office in a down-town office building in Newark, N. J. This "one-man Institute", according to their literature, has no faculty except Father Oesterreicher, and no students. Father Oesterreicher was born a so-called or self-styled "Jew" and became a convert to Catholicism. I have had the pleasure of hearing him talk on many occasions. Addresses by Father Oesterreicher and literature by mail are the principal activities of the "Institute of Judaeo-Christian Studies". Father Oesterreicher also plans to publish books and circulate them throughout the world, in large quantities.

Father Oesterreicher leaves no stones unturned to convince Catholics that "Judaeo-Christian" is a combination of two words that are synonyms theologically. Nothing could be further from the truth. Father Oesterreicher impresses that viewpoint upon his Catholic audiences. Father Oesterreicher talks to Catholic audiences only, so far as I am able to tell. In his addresses Father Oesterreicher impresses upon Catholics the opinion he personally holds on the question of the dependence of the Christian faith upon so-called "Judaism". His audiences depart Father Osterreicher's addresses very much confused.

It would make better Catholics out of Father Oesterreicher's audiences if he would "sell" Jesus and the Catholic Church rather than try to "sell" so-called "Judaism" to his audiences. Well-planned and well-financed publicity by so-called or self-styled "Jews" manages to keep Christians well informed on the subject of so-called "Judaism". If Father Oesterreicher would concentrate upon "selling" Jesus and the Christian faith to audiences of so-called or self-styled "Jews" he would be doing more towards realizing the objectives of Christian effort. The activities of this "one-man Institute" are somewhat of a deep mystery. But I am certain that Monsignor McNulty will never allow the "Institute of Judaeo-Christian Studies" to bring discredit upon the fine record of Seton Hall as one of the foremost Catholic universities anywhere. But it will bear watching, and Monsignor McNulty will always appreciate constructive comment.

The word "anti-Semitism" is another word which should be eliminated from the English language. "Anti-Semitism" serves only one purpose today. It is used as a "smear word". When so-called or self-styled "Jews" feel that anyone opposes any of their objectives they discredit their victims by applying the word "anti-Semite" or "anti-Semitic" through all the channels they have at their command and under their control. I can speak with great authority on that subject. Because so-called or self-styled "Jews" were unable to disprove my public statements in 1946 with regard to the situation in Palestine, they spent millions of dollars to "smear" me as an "anti-Semite" hoping thereby to discredit me in the eyes of the public who were very much interested in what I had to say. Until 1946 I was a "little saint" to all so-called or self-styled "Jews". When I disagreed with them publicly on the Zionist intentions in Palestine I became suddenly "Anti-Semite No. 1".

It is disgraceful to watch the Christian clergy take up the use of the word "anti-Semitism". They should know better. They know that "anti-Semitism" is a meaningless word in the sense it is used today. They know the correct word is "Judaeophobe". "Anti-Semite" was developed into the "smear-word" it is today because "Semite" is associated with Jesus in the minds of Christians. Christians are accessories in the destruction of the Christian faith by tolerating the use of the smear-word "anti-Semitic" to silence by the most intolerant forms of persecution employing that smear word Christians who oppose the evil conspirators.

It no doubt grieves you as much as it grieves me, my dear Dr. Goldstein, to see our nation's moral standards sink to new all-time lows day by day. Of that there is very little doubt. The moral standards of this nation in political, economic, social and spiritual fields are the factors which determine the position we will occupy in world affairs. We will be judged on that basis from afar by the other 94% of the world's total population. Our 6% of the world's total population will succeed or fail in its efforts to retain world leadership by our moral standards because in the last analysis they influence the attitudes and activities of the nation. The moral standards are the crucible in which the nation's character is refined and molded. The end product will never be any better than the ingredients used. It is something to think about.

There is much for which this Christian country can still feel very proud. But there is also much for which we cannot feel proud. A correct diagnosis of our nation's rapidly deteriorating moral standards in all walks of life will reveal the cause as the nation's current psychosis to concentrate primarily on how to (1) "make MORE money" and (2) "have MORE fun". How many persons do you personally know who include among their daily duties service and sacrifice in the defense against its enemies of that priceless birthright which is the God-given heritage of all those blessed to be born Americans? What services? What sacrifices?

With very few exceptions this generation seems to regard everything as secondary to our accountability to unborn generations for our generation's breach of the faith and betrayal of our trust to posterity. The sabotage of our nation's moral standards is more incidental to the program of that inimical conspiracy than accidental in the continued march of mankind towards an easier existence. The guidance and control of this nation's place in history has gravitated by default into the hands of those persons least worthy of that trusteeship. This notable achievement by them is their reward for their success in obtaining effective and numerous Christian "male prostitutes" to "front" for them. Too many of these efficacious Christian "male prostitutes" are scattered throughout the nation in public affairs for the security of the Christian faith and the nation's political, social and economic stability.

A "male prostitute" is a male who offers the faculties of his anatomy from the neck up for hire to anyone who will pay his "asking price" exactly as the female of the same species offers the facilities of her anatomy from the neck down to anyone who will pay her "asking price". Thousands of these pseudo-Christian "male-prostitutes" circulate freely unrecognized in all walks of life proudly pandering pernicious propaganda for pecuniary profit and political power. They are the "dog in the manger". The corroding effect of their subtle intrigue is slowly but surely disintegrating the moral fiber of the nation. This danger to the Christian faith cannot be overestimated. This peril to the nation should not be under- estimated. The Christian clergy must remain alerted to it.

The international "crime of crimes" of all history, that reprehensible iniquity in which this nation played the major role, was committed in Palestine almost totally as a result of the interference of the United States in that situation on behalf solely of the Zionist world-wide organization with its headquarters in New York City. The interference of the United States in that situation on behalf of the aggressors illustrates the power exerted upon the domestic and foreign policies of this government by the "male prostitutes" fearlessly functioning on behalf of the Zionist conspirators. It is the blackest page in our history.

The responsibility for that un-Christian, non-Christian and anti-Christian "cause" can be honestly deposited on the door-step of the Christian clergy. They must assume the full guilt for that inhumane and unholy crime committed in the name of Christian "charity". Sunday after Sunday, year in and year out, the Christian clergy dinned into the ears of 150,000,000 Christians who go to church regularly that Christians must regard it as their "Christian duty" to support the Zionist conspiracy for the conquest of Palestine. Well, we "sowed a wind", now we will "reap a whirlwind".

The 150,000,000 Christians in the United States were "high pressured" by the Christian clergy to give their unqualified support to the Zionist program to "repatriate" to their "homeland" in Palestine the so-called or self-styled "Jews" in eastern Europe who were the descendants of the Khazars. Christians were exhorted by the Christian clergy to regard the so-called or self-styled "Jews" in eastern Europe as God's "chosen people" and Palestine as their "Promised Land". But they knew better all the time. It was a case of cupidity not stupidity you can be sure.

As a direct result of the activities of the "male prostitutes" on behalf of the Zionist program, and contrary to all international law, to justice and to equity, anything to the contrary notwithstanding, the 150,000,000 Christians in the United States, with few exceptions, demanded that the Congress of the United States use the prestige and the power of this nation, diplomatic, economic and military, to guarantee the successful outcome of the Zionist program for the conquest of Palestine. This was done and the Zionists conquered Palestine. We are responsible.

It is a well-established and an undeniable historic fact that the active participation of the United States in the conquest of Palestine, on behalf of the Zionists, was the factor responsible for the conquest of Palestine by the Zionists.

Without the active participation of the United States on behalf of the Zionists it is certain that the Zionists would never have attempted the conquest of Palestine by force of arms. Palestine today would be an independent sovereign country under a form of government established by self-determination of the lawful and legal Palestinians. This was aborted by the payment of countless millions of dollars to Christian "male prostitutes" by Zionists on a scale difficult for the uninitiated to even imagine.

With your kind permission anticipated, I beg to respectfully and sincerely now submit to you here my comments on several passages in your latest article which appeared in the September issue of the A.P.J. Bulletin under the headline "News and Views of Jews". Deep down in my heart, my dear Dr. Goldstein, I truly feel that I can make a modest contribution towards the big success I wish you in the valuable work you are attempting, under such discouraging handicaps. My reactions to what you state in your article may prove helpful to you. My comments here were conceived in that spirit. May I suggest that you favor them with your consideration accordingly. I feel that you may be so close to the "trees" that you cannot see the "forest" in its true perspective. You may find a genuinely sincere outsider's point of view helpful to you in orienting your yesterday's attitudes to today's realities and to tomorrow's seemingly certain probabilities. I believe you will.

You realize, my dear Dr. Goldstein, that all "Laws of Nature" are irrevocable. "Laws of Nature" can neither be amended, suspended or repealed regardless how we fell about them. One of these "Laws of Nature" is fundamentally the basic reason "WHY JEWS BECOME CATHOLICS", the subtitle in your article which attracted my attention. The "Law of Nature" to which I refer is the law that "TO EVERY ACTION THERE IS AN EQUAL AND OPPOSITE REACTIONS." In my respectful opinion that "Law of Nature is the alpha and omega of all questions as to "WHY JEWS BECOME CATHOLICS."

In your article you make this mystery sound very complicated. However, it really is very simple. The so-called or self-styled "Jews" who become Catholics today are subconsciously reacting to that "Law of Nature". The conversion to Catholicism of the so-called or self-styled "Jews" is the "EQUAL AND OPPOSITE REACTION" of that "Law of Nature". Their conversion is a "REACTION" not an "ACTION". Can you any longer doubt that after reading these facts?

Catholicism has proven itself spiritually the "EQUAL AND OPPOSITE REACTION" of the religious worship practiced today under the name "Judaism", and prior to that name under the names "Talmudism" and "Pharisaism". What is spiritually conspicuous in Catholicism is conspicuous by its absence in so-called "Judaism". What is spiritually conspicuous in so-called "Judaism" is conspicuous by its absence in Catholicism, thank God. Anything which may be said by anyone to the contrary notwithstanding, Catholicism and so-called "Judaism" are at the opposite extremes of the spiritual spectrum.

Our subconscious mind never sleeps. It remains awake all the while the conscious mind is asleep. This subconscious mind of so-called or self-styled "Jews" is "WHY JEWS BECOME CATHOLICS". The more spiritually sensitive subconscious minds of the so-called or self-styled "Jews" for 2000 years has been seeking a spiritually secure beach-head as a refuge from the terror of the Talmud. After a lifetime breathing the atmosphere of the Talmud so-called or self-styled "Jews" found Catholicism a wholesome and refreshing change of spiritual climate. They could not resist the spiritual force of the "EQUAL AND OPPOSITE REACTION" WHICH ATTRACTED THEM TO CATHOLICISM.

Catholicism supplied a sacred sanctuary for the more spiritually sensitive subconscious mind of the so-called or self- styled "Jew" seeking security in his escape from the Talmud. Before sailing into the safe port of Catholicism the subconscious mind of the more spiritually sensitive so-called or self-styled "Jews" would embark upon that voyage of their more courageous co-religionists but for one reason. They fear reprisals by their co-religionists.

In your article you mention just a few of the many penalties imposed by reactionary so-called or self-styled "Jews" upon their co-religionists who become converts to Catholicism. Conversion to Catholicism has even deprived many former so-called or self-styled "Jews" from earning their living. Many families faced starvation for that reason. A convert to Catholicism must be ready and willing to suffer the economic, social and political hardships his former co-religionists will make him pay as the price for the spiritual wealth he will acquire with conversion to Catholicism.

Investigation by you will convince you that so-called or self-styled "Jews" never turn spiritually to Catholicism "BECAUSE SUCH WAS THE JEWISH RELIGION: BECAUSE SUCH IS THE CATHOLIC RELIGION", as you state in your article. A so-called or self-styled "Jew" might question the wisdom of conversion from the original to a copy of the original. Inasmuch as so-called "Judaism" is a modern name for "Talmudism", and "Talmudism" is a name given to the ancient practice of "Pharisaism", how can you reconcile what you state that ". . . SUCH WAS THE JEWISH RELIGION: . . . SUCH IS THE CATHOLIC RELIGION".

Several so-called or self-styled "Jews" who were recently converted to Catholicism are my personal friends. Not one of those whom I have asked became a Catholic because they felt "THE CATHOLIC CHURCH IS THE

JEWISH CHURCH GLORIFIED", as you state in your article. What "JEWISH CHURCH" they ask me? I am unable to answer. What "JEWISH CHURCH" I ask you? "Pharisaism"? "Talmudism"? Surely you would not venture the opinion that the Catholic Church is "Pharisaism" or "Talmudism" now "GLORIFIED" as Catholicism, would you?

It must be quite apparent to you now that so-called or self-styled "Jews" who became converts to Catholicism do not believe that the Catholic Church, as you state in your article, "IS THE CHURCH OF JEWISH CONVERTS AND THEIR DESCENDANTS". They do not regard Jesus as a "CONVERT" to the Catholic Church. You include Jesus as a "CONVERT" to the Catholic Church, in your article. In your article you state, "FIRST CAME CHRIST, THE JEW OF JEWS". I never heard that designation before. Is it original? Nor will converted so-called or self-styled "Jews" concur at all with "THEN CAME THE APOSTLES, ALL JEWS", as you also state in your article. There is unquestionably too big an area of disagreement here to disregard the views of those who have become converts to Catholicism. Nor can these converts to Catholicism be made to believe as truth "THEN CAME THE THOUSANDS OF THE FIRST MEMBERS OF THE CATHOLIC CHURCH, WHO WERE JEWS", as you state in your article under discussion here.

My dear Dr. Goldstein, as a former so-called or self-styled "Jew" for almost half your life, when you became a convert to Catholicism did you do so for the reasons you state in your article "WHY JEWS BECOME CATHOLICS"? That would be difficult for me to believe in spite of the further statements you make in your article "IN FACT THERE WOULD NOT HAVE BEEN A CATHOLIC CHURCH WERE IT NOT FOR THE JEWS". That statement appears incredible in view of incontestable facts, but these facts may not have been available to you when you made it.

If so-called or self-styled "Jews" believed what you state in your article they would undoubtedly prefer to stay put spiritually in their "JEWISH CHURCH", by which you mean no doubt so-called "Judaism". They would query why Catholics expected them to leave their "JEWISH CHURCH" to enter the Catholic Church. It might appear more logical to expect Catholics to return to the original of the Catholic Church, the "JEWISH CHURCH", or so-called "Judaism". On the basis of what you state, that would not be inconsistent.

You take away my breath when you further state "CATHOLICISM WOULD NOT EXIST WERE IT NOT FOR JUDAISM". That leaves very little for me to say after writing these 62 pages of facts and comments. In a certain sense there is certain sense to what you state if you feel that the existence of so-called "Judaism", in the time of Jesus and since then, created the necessity for the existence of Catholicism. But in no sense can the Catholic Church be adjudicated the projection of "Pharisaism", "Talmudism", or so-called "Judaism".

We should get together in person to go into this matter more fully. I hope you will extend that privilege to me in the not too distant future. In closing this letter I sincerely request that you bear in mind while reading this letter Galatians, 4:16, "Am I therefore become your enemy, because I tell you the truth?" And to this I add, "I hope not". I hope that we shall continue to be the very best of friends. If the Christian faith is to be rescued from its dedicated enemies we must all join hands and form a "human lifeline". We must pull together, not in different directions. We must "bury the hatchet" but not in each other's heads.

Looking forward with pleasant anticipation to the delight of meeting with you in person whenever you find it convenient and agreeable for yourself, and awaiting your early reply for which I take this opportunity to thank you in advance, and with best wishes for your continued good health and success, please believe me to be,


Most respectfully and very sincerely,

*Benjamin H. Freedman*

# Hidden Tyrany

The names of Presidents Woodrow Wilson, Franklin D. Roosevelt, Harry S. Truman, Dwight D. Eisenhower, John F. Kennedy, Lyndon B. Johnson and Richard M. Nixon will certainly be found one day inscribed in big red letters in the official annals of the rise and fall of the United States. These seven masters of deception incurred their guilt by debasing their solemn oaths of office on behalf of undisclosed domestic and foreign principals without any apparent qualms or misgivings, to enhance their political fortunes totally oblivious of the threat to United States security and survival. These seven masters of deception knowingly and willingly in effect and in fact "poisoned the wells" of security and survival for the United States. Without any evident scruples, they individually betrayed the sacred traditions enshrined in the letter and spirit of their oaths of office, that precious heritage bequeathed to each of these seven masters of deception as successors to that high office exalted by the immortalized first president of the United States, the venerated George Washington. The disclosures which follow here are now revealed for the first time anywhere. They now expose for the first time to the grass roots population of the United States the secret un-American, non-American and anti-American strategy to which these seven masters of deception knowingly subscribed. The uninhibited practice of that strategy by these seven masters of deception is primarily responsible for desperate predicament in which the United States today finds itself in the Middle East. Very early in their political careers, these seven masters of deception by their determination acquired their proficient skill in detecting on which side their political bread was buttered. Their remarkable perfection in that skill provides the answer to why these seven masters of deception went so far and so fast in so few years in the political world in which they moved. Throughout their political careers these seven masters of deception demonstrated that political shrewdness invariably identified with the immoral dogma of 20th century politicians who preach and practice "any means justifies all ends." Accordingly, future grass roots populations of the United

States will one day find inscribed in the history of the rise and fall of the United States the verdict that the "means" today advocated by these seven masters of deception were primarily responsible for the "end" of the United States. It is today a well recognized fact of life in political circles in the United States that the censorship exercised today by Zionists over the media for mass information constitutes a virtual monopoly. It is likewise today a well recognized fact of life in political circles in the United States since President Wilson won his first election in 1912 as president of the United States, that elections in the United States are seldom won or lost today based upon the candidates' qualification for office. Elections in the United States since 1912 are won or lost on the battlefields of the media for mass information by character assassination. Zionist ownership of media for mass information, or by Zionist control exercised by some devious corporate device in effect and in fact censors the news and editorial policies of as the leading daily and Sunday newspapers, all the weekly and monthly news magazines, all leading radio and television stations and networks, the entire motion picture industry, the entire entertainment world and the entire book publishing industry, in effect and in fact the entire complex of media for mass information in the United States, truly a brainwashing monopoly.

## Talmudist Jews Control News and Editorial Policies of Mass Media

As a result of that condition in the United States, for approximately the past fifty years the grass roots population of the United States has only read, heard and seen what passed Zionist censorship and best served Zionist objectives, instead of reading, hearing and seeing what best served the interests of the grass roots population of the United States. The Zionist-ruled media for mass information in the United States never informed the grass roots population of the United States how and why President Woodrow Wilson led the United States into the desperate predicament in which the United States today finds itself in the Middle East. In their consideration recently of the alleged theft of the so-called Pentagon Papers, the United States Supreme Court declared "the public has a right to know the truth." The Supreme Court should have said "the public has a right to know the WHOLE truth." The reason half-truths often are more harmful than lies. The United States declared war against Germany on April 6, 1917. On April 2, 1917 President Wilson addressed both houses of Congress and pleaded with them to declare war against Germany. President Wilson's appeal to Congress to declare war against Germany in effect and in fact was primarily President Wilson's liquidation of his obligation to his blackmailers. The following incontestable facts confirm that conclusion beyond all question of any doubt. President Wilson's hand trembled as he read his address. The members of Congress present had no reason to suspect why President Wilson's hand trembled. By the time the grass roots population finish reading this, they will know the reason President Wilson's hand trembled as he read his message to Congress. By the time President Wilson finished reading his appeal to Congress, many of his listeners were in tears but not for the reason the grass roots population of the United States today will be in tears when they finish reading this manuscript. When President Wilson asked Congress to declare war against Germany, President Wilson was in effect and in fact conspiring to pay the debt he obligated himself to pay to the Zionists. Congress only declared war against Germany because President Wilson informed Congress that a German submarine had sunk the S.S. Sussex in the English Channel in violation of international law and that United States citizens aboard the S.S. Sussex had perished with the ship. After General Pershing's troops were fighting in Europe, the hoax was exposed. The alleged sinking of the S.S. Sussex was used as the "pretext" to justify a declaration of war against Germany by the United States. The S.S. Sussex had not been sunk and no United States citizens had lost their lives. The United States was now at war in Europe as Great Britain's ally. That is what Great Britain and the Talmudists ("Jews") of the world conspired to achieve in their crooked diplomatic underworld. The discovery of the hoax by the British Navy shocked many honorable Englishmen. A large segment of the British public were shocked to learn the S.S. Sussex had not been sunk. The S.S. Sussex was available for anyone to visit who might care to do so to see the S.S. Sussex for themselves with their own eyes. In that war the United States mobilized 4,734,991 men to serve in the armed forces, of whom 115,516 were killed and 202,002 were either injured or maimed for life. The Right Honorable Francis Neilson, a member of Parliament, wrote a book in England called Makers of War (pp. 149-150). Mr. Neilson's book created such a sensation that Mr. Neilson was compelled to resign his seat in Parliament. Things became so intolerable for Mr. Neilson in Great Britain as a result of the exposures in his book that he was compelled for his personal safety to flee from his home in Great Britain and to make his home in the United States. In Mr. Neilson's book Makers of War (pp. 149-150), he discloses many unsuspected and undisclosed reasons for the outbreak of World War I in Europe in August 1914. With reference to the alleged sinking of the S.S. Sussex in the English Channel, Mr. Neilson emphasizes: "In America, Woodrow Wilson, desperate to find a pretext to enter the war, found it at last in the 'sinking' of the Sussex in mid-channel. Someone invented a yarn that American lives had been lost. With thus excuse he went to Congress for a declaration of war. Afterwards, the Navy found that the Sussex had not been sunk, and that no lives had been lost." This author crossed the English Channel many times on the S.S. Sussex. The alleged sinking of the S.S. Sussex was the figment of an over-worked Zionist imagination. The alleged sinking of the S.S. Sussex was conceived in the imagination of a Zionist to facilitate the purpose planned and successfully executed.

### President Wilson Blackmailed

Shortly after President Wilson's first inauguration, he received a visitor in the White House by the name of Mr. Samuel Untermeyer. Mr. Untermeyer was a prominent New York City attorney who contributed generously to the National Democratic Committee that installed President Wilson in the White House in Washington in the 1912 election. Mr. Untermeyer was a very welcome guest and President Wilson was very glad to welcome him to the White House. They had met before during the campaign. Mr. Untermeyer surprised President Wilson when he finally stated what brought him to the

White House. Mr. Untermeyer informed President Wilson that he had been retained to bring a breach of promise action against President Wilson. Mr. Untermeyer informed President Wilson that his client was willing to accept $40,000 in lieu of commencing the breach of promise action. Mr. Untermeyer's client was the former wife of a Professor at Princeton University at the same time President Wilson was a professor at Princeton University. Mr. Untermeyer produced a packet of letters from his pocket, written by President Wilson to his colleague's wife when they were neighbors at Princeton University. These letters established the illicit relationship which had existed between President Wilson and the wife of his colleague neighbor. He had written many endearing letters to her, many of which she never destroyed. President Wilson acknowledged his authorship of the letters after examining a few of them. President Wilson left Princeton University to become the Governor of New Jersey. In 1912 he was elected to his first term as president of the United States. In the interim, President Wilson's former sweetheart had divorced her husband and married again. Her second husband was a resident in Washington with a grown son who was in the employ of one of the leading banks in Washington. Mr. Untermeyer explained to President Wilson that his former sweetheart was very fond of her husband's son. He explained that this son was in financial trouble and suddenly needed $40,000 as he told the story, to liquidate a pressing liability to the bank for which he worked. The details are not relevant here except that the son needed the $40,000 badly and quickly. President Wilson's former sweetheart thought that Wilson was the logical prospect for that $40,000 to help her husband's son. Mr. Untermeyer visited President Wilson at the White House to break the news to him about the breach of promise action being considered. Wilson expressed himself as very fortunate that his former sweetheart went to Mr. Untermeyer to seek his assistance. The publicity could have proven very embarrassing to President Wilson if his former sweetheart had instead consulted a Republican attorney. President Wilson quickly set Mr. Untermeyer's mind at rest by informing him that he did not have $40,000 available for any purpose. Mr. Untermeyer suggested that President Wilson should think the matter over and said he would return in a few days to discuss the matter further. Mr. Untermeyer used the next few days in Washington looking into the credibility of the son's story about his pressing need for $40,000 to liquidate a pressing liability. He learned that the son's story was not misrepresented in any way to his mother by her son. Mr. Untermeyer returned to President Wilson a few days later as they had agreed. President Wilson did not hesitate to inform Mr. Untermeyer that he did not have the $40,000 to pay his blackmailer. President Wilson appeared irritated. Mr. Untermeyer considered the matter a few Moments and then volunteered a solution to President Wilson for his problem. Mr. Untermeyer volunteered to give President Wilson's former sweetheart the $40,000 out of his own pocket on one condition: that Wilson promise Untermeyer to appoint to the first vacancy on the United States Supreme Court a nominee to be recommended to Wilson by Untermeyer. Without further talk, President Wilson accepted Mr. Untermeyer's generous offer and Mr. Untermeyer promptly paid the $40,000 in currency to President Wilson's former sweetheart. The contemplated breach of promise suit was never heard of after that. Mr. Untermeyer retained in his possession permanently the packet of letters to insure against any similar attempt at some future time. President Wilson was most grateful to Mr. Untermeyer for everything he was doing to solve problem. Mr. Untermeyer was a man of great wealth. The law firm in New York of which he was the leading partner, Messrs. Guggenheim, Untermeyer and Marshall, is still today one of the nation's most prominent and most prosperous law firms. Mr. Untermeyer organized the Bethlehem Steel Company for his friend, Mr. Charles M. Schwab, who resigned from the United States Steel Company to form his company in competition with it.

## Justice Brandeis — The Pay Off

As anyone might reasonably suspect, Mr. Untermeyer must have had something in mind when he agreed to pay President Wilson's former sweetheart $40,000 out of his own pocket. He paid the money out of his own pocket in the hope that it might bring to pass a dream close to his heart — a Talmudist ("Jew") on the

United States Supreme Court on which none had ever served. The day soon arrived when President Wilson was presented with the necessity of appointing a new member of the United States Supreme Court. Mr. Untermeyer recommended Louis Dembitz Brandeis for the vacancy, who was immediately appointed by Wilson. President Wilson and Justice Brandeis became unusually intimate friends. Justice Brandeis knew the circumstances of his appointment to the Supreme Court by President Wilson. In 1914 Justice Brandeis was the most prominent and most politically influential of all Zionists in the United States. As a Justice of the United States Supreme Court, Brandeis was in a better position than ever before to be of service to Talmudists ("Jews") both at home and abroad. The first opportunity to perform a great service for his Zionist followers soon became available to Brandeis. Justice Brandeis volunteered his opinion to President Wilson that the sinking of the S.S. Sussex by a German submarine in the English Channel with the loss of lives of United States citizens justified the declaration of war against Germany by the United States. Relying to a great extent upon the legal opinion of Justice Brandeis, President Wilson addressed both houses of Congress on April 2, 1917. He appealed to Congress to declare war against Germany and they did on April 7, 1917. After the October 1916 agreement was concluded between the British War Cabinet and the World Zionist Organization, the Talmudists throughout the world were hopeful that an international incident would soon occur to Justify a declaration of war against Germany by the United States. The declaration of war against Germany by the United States guaranteed the Talmudists throughout the world that Palestine was to be turned over to them upon the defeat of Germany. The defeat of Germany was certain if the United States could be railroaded into the war in Europe as Great Britain's ally. Prior to the October 1916 London Agreement, Talmudists throughout the world were pro-German. The German Emancipation Edict of 1822 guaranteed Talmudists in Germany all civil rights enjoyed by Germans. Every country in Europe had quotas for Talmudists. The quota systems had existed for centuries in all European countries. Under the quota system in European countries, Talmudists were limited in all activities to a small percentage of the Christian population of the country. The quota systems applied to all occupations. After the Emancipation Edict in 1822, Germany was the only country in Europe which did not place restrictions on Talmudists under a quota system limiting their civil rights. Talmudists throughout the world were informed by cable from London about the October 1916 London Agreement. That information transformed them from pro-German to pro-British. Great Britain placed at the disposal of Talmudists in London their secret codes and worldwide cable facilities to inform Talmudists throughout the world about Great Britain's pledge to turn over Palestine to them as compensation for railroading the United States into the war in Europe as Great Britain's ally in their war against Germany. Talmudists enlisted in great numbers in October 1916 in Great Britain's Department of Defense. Their purpose was to facilitate transforming Talmudists throughout the world from pro-German to pro-British. After the London Agreement was concluded, Great Britain left no stone unturned to impress Talmudists in London with the necessity of immediately notifying Talmudists throughout the world about Great Britain's pledge to turn over Palestine to them for their future sovereign Zionist state. Guided by the recommendation of Justice Brandeis that the sinking of the S.S. Sussex justified a declaration of war under international law against Germany by the United States, President Wilson addressed a joint session of both houses of Congress on April 2, 1917. In that address President Wilson pleaded with Congress to declare war against Germany. Congress met on April 6, 1917, and declared war against Germany without justification. On April 6, 1917, President Wilson and Justice Brandeis knew something the grass roots population of the United States did not know — they knew full particulars about the October 1916 London Agreement. They also knew the declaration of war against Germany by the United States activated this agreement and that Talmudists of the world would not have to wait long for Palestine, their sovereign Zionist state, if their plan worked. On this same day, Wilson and Brandeis knew something else the grass roots population of the United States did not know — they knew that the declaration of war by the United States against Germany discharged

President Wilson from his obligation to his blackmailers. Wilson's declaration of war was to satisfy his commitment to his blackmailers. There was seldom any address made to Congress that stirred the people of the United States, and the world, as did President Wilson's April 2, 1917, plea to Congress to declare war against Germany. Wilson was aware when he addressed Congress that Germany had not committed any act against the United States which justified a declaration of war by the United States against Germany under international law. This author at that time knew President Wilson was informed to that effect before he made his plea to Congress.

## Prime Minister Lloyd George – A Zionist Tool

There were great numbers of Talmudists in the United States who questioned the reality of the October 1916 London Agreement. They found it extremely difficult to believe that Great Britain would promise to turn over Palestine to them as compensation for railroading the United States into the war in Europe as Great Britain's ally. These Talmudists could not believe that Great Britain would promise anything to anyone that Great Britain did not own as compensation. That appeared inconceivable to Talmudists familiar with Great Britain's reputation for respect of property rights under their laws. To overcome doubts that existed in the minds of Talmudists in the United States, Prime Minister Lloyd George immediately sent Mr. Josiah Wedgewood to the United States. Mr. Wedgewood was one of the most respected and dedicated members of Parliament. Prime Minister Lloyd George, a rabid well-known Zionist, was unexpectedly appointed Prime Minister on December 4, 1916. He rushed Mr. Wedgewood to the United States on December 5, 1916, under pressure by Talmudists in London. The prime minister whom Lloyd George succeeded was unsympathetic Toward Zionist objectives. He was replaced at that time because Zionists could not rule him. Great Britain was helpless in October 1916. It was seriously considering surrender to Germany. Germany had made several peace offers to Great Britain earlier to discontinue the war. Mr. Lloyd George considered Mr. Wedgewood's hasty trip to the United States vital to Great Britain's survival. Mr. Wedgewood went to the United States with documented evidence proving the reality of the October 1916 London Agreement with the Talmudists.

## Colonel House – a Conspiring Enigma

Mr. Wedgewood arrived in the United States on December 23, 1916. Upon his arrival he was met at the pier by Colonel Edward Mandel House, President Wilson's closest personal friend and most trusted adviser. Col. House in early life negotiated cotton purchases in the United States for Rothschild interests in Great Britain. Col. House did not claim or disclaim his Talmudist ancestry to this author. He had arranged with Mr. Wedgewood to live in his apartment on 54th Street during his stay in the United States. Col. House quickly made arrangements for the meeting at which Mr. Wedgewood was to prove the reality of the October 1916 London Agreement. The meeting was to be held on Sunday afternoon, December 25, 1916, at the old Hotel Savoy at 59th Street and Fifth Avenue in New Yolk City. There were fifty-one invited Talmudists present there when Col. House introduced Mr. Wedgewood to the audience. Mr. Wedgewood then presided. Mr. Wedgewood presented evidence there that left no doubt in the minds of the fifty-one Talmudists present about the reality of the October 1916 London Agreement. On behalf of Mr. Lloyd George, Mr. Wedgewood further vouched for the reality of Great Britain pledge that Palestine would be turned over to Talmudists of the world by Great Britain upon the defeat of Germany as compensation for railroading the United States into the war in Europe as Great Britain's ally. After concluding the October 1916 London Agreement, Talmudists in England were invited by Great Britain to take an increasingly active participation in Great Britain's Department of Defense for the duration of the war. The Talmudists who accepted the invitation were trained as experts in the use of Great Britain's codes and Great Britain's worldwide diplomatic cable facilities. The available data in Great Britain's archives for World War I will dispel all existing doubt whether the information cabled to Washington from London alleging the sinking of the S.S. Sussex and the loss of United States lives was the invention of Talmudists in London in Great Britain's Department of

Defense to facilitate and expedite railroading the United States into the war in Europe as Great Britain's ally. The hoax was discovered by the British Navy. It was also confirmed by other equally reliable sources for information on the subject by qualified united States experts. The reality of the October 1916 London Agreement was known to the Germans shortly after it was concluded, in fact, on the same day. Germany thereafter exercised great care both on land and on sea not to commit any act which, under international law, could provide the United States with justification to declare war against Germany. German military and naval commanders leaned over backwards in their effort not to provide the United States with that justification and they were successful. In the crisis in October 1916, Germans had reason to feel if the war in Europe continued a few more months without the entrance of the United States into the war, that Great Britain would be compelled to surrender to Germany by circumstances beyond Great Britain's power to control. Germany made another peace offer to Great Britain in October 1916. Great Britain this time welcomed the offer but it was also declined like several previous peace offers. In referring to the declaration of war against Germany by the United States, Sir Winston Churchill said in an interview with a prominent editor, published in Scribner's Commentator in 1936, that he "could never understand why he put us in 1917," referring to President Wilson. In that interview Sir Winston Churchill stated further: "America should have minded her own business and stayed out of the World War. If you hadn't entered the war the Allies would have made peace with Germany in the spring of 1917. Had we made peace there would have been no collapse of Russia followed by Communism, no breakdown in Italy followed by Fascism, and Germany would not have signed the Versailles Treaty, which has enthroned Nazism in Germany. If America had stayed out of the war, all of these 'isms' wouldn't be sweeping the continent of Europe and breaking down parliamentary government, and if England made peace early in 1917, it would have saved over one million British, French, American and other lives." Germany's peace offer to Great Britain asked for neither indemnities nor reparations. Germany offered to restore the territorial status and the political independence of every country with whom Great Britain was at war, as they existed in August 1914 when the war in Europe started. Germany demanded no benefits.

## Talmudist Jews Select America's Ally for First World War

Germany's October 1916 peace offer was on the table before the British War Cabinet; it needed only one signature to end the war. Great Britain would have quickly accepted Germany's peace offer if the World Zionist Organization had not interfered. The British War Cabinet was then taking their instructions from Talmudists in London. When the British War Cabinet decided to accept Germany's peace offer, the World Zionist Organization offered to railroad the United States into the war in Europe as Great Britain's ally if Great Britain promised the Talmudists of the world Palestine as compensation after Germany's defeat with the United States as an ally. Talmudist pressure in London and New York prevailed. President Wilson had little choice in the matter, it seemed. He was the captive of circumstances in his early life that could not be altered. His April 2, 1917, address to Congress was about to decide the fate of the world. Congress, without hesitation, declared war against Germany for him. The Germans attributed their crushing defeat in World War I to the entry of the United States into the war in Europe as Great Britain's ally. Germany considered the October 1916 London Agreement a stab in the back by Talmudists of the world. In view of the Emancipation Edict in Germany in 1822, Germans regarded the London Agreement as a double-cross by Talmudists in Germany. Quota systems then existed in all other countries in Europe. There was no quota system in Germany after the Emancipation Edict of 1822 for Talmudists.

## Talmudist Jews Promote Germans Victory, Then Stab them in the Back

The Kaiser provided the World Zionist Organization with the offices for their world headquarters in Berlin. He, his family and government officials were constantly extending assistance to Theodore Herzl. Germany extended opportunities to Talmudists not available in other European countries. The Kaiser himself arranged the personal meeting between the Sultan of the Ottoman Empire and Theodore Herzl. Bleichroeder & Company in Berlin were the private bankers of the Kaiser's family for generations. They were Talmudists. Warburg & Company of Hamburg were the world's largest merchant bankers. They were Talmudists. The head of the German General Electric Company, then the world's largest industrial enterprise, was a Talmudist. The head of the Hamburg-American and North German Lloyd steamship companies, the two largest steamship companies in the world, second only to the Cunard Line, was a Talmudist. Countless prominent German industrialists, bankers and merchants were Talmudists. The attitude of Germans towards Talmudists in Germany and throughout the world worsened much after the October 1916 stab in the back by Talmudists. Mr. Samuel Landman, the secretary of the World Zionist Organization in London from 1917 to 1922, wrote in his Great Britain, the Jews and Palestine, published in London in 1936, on page six: "The fact that it was Jewish help that brought the U.S.A. into the war on the side of the Allies has rankled ever since in German — especially Nazi — minds and has contributed in no small measure to the prominence which anti-Semitism occupied in the Nazi programme." The sentiments of prominent German leaders were expressed in the Jewish Daily Bulletin of New York City on October 30, 1934, in an article reprinted on page three from the Jewish Telegraphic Agency dispatch from Berlin which stated: "The New Germany persists toward the complete extermination of the Jew because it was Jews who instigated the United States to enter the World War, accomplishing the defeat of Germany, and who later caused the inflation in Germany, Herr Richard Kunze, a leading Nazi Parliament figure, declared at a mass meeting in Magdeburg yesterday." Talmudists throughout the world made bad matters worse on August 7, 1933, when they declared their "holy war" to destroy the German nation "by destroying their export trade upon which their very existence depends." Under the leadership of Mr. Samuel Untermeyer, Talmudists of the world declared a world boycott on all German goods and services. They asked their "Christian friends" to join their worldwide boycott of German goods and services.

Mr. Samuel Untermeyer arranged for the "International Boycott Conference" in Amsterdam in July 1933. There he was elected the president of the "World Jewish Economic Federation." Talmudists throughout the world had tried in vain since 1919 to silence German resentment against them for railroading the United States into the war in Europe without justification or provocation by the United States as Great Britain's ally. Talmudists were held responsible for Germany's defeat and for every disadvantage that resulted from that defeat. The New York Times of August 7, 1933, published the Talmudists' declaration of their "holy war" against Germany in a three-column report of Mr. Untermeyer's address to the nation from the Columbia Broadcasting Company's studio on the night of his arrival home from Europe. Mr. Untermeyer, among other things, stated: "...holy war...in which we are embarked..it is a war which must be waged unremittingly...the Jews are the aristocrats of the world... the economic boycott against all German goods, shipping and services...boycott is our only really effective weapon...bring the German people to their senses by destroying their export trade on which their very existence depends...we shall force them to learn... it is not sufficient that you buy no goods in Germany...you must refuse to deal with any merchant or shopkeeper who sells any German-made goods...we will drive the last nail in the coffin..." That statement was made on August 7, 1933, when not a hair on the head of a Talmudist in Germany had been touched. Germany was plunged into a depression difficult to describe in a few words, Germany's export business suddenly ending as if by magic. Talmudists hoped that way to stop Germans from continuing to talk about why they lost the war. Talmudists in Germany were finding it difficult to live that down. Germans then felt the way Sir Winston Churchill in 1936 expressed himself about the entry of the United States into World War I in 1917.

## Zionist Worldwide Boycott Against German Merchandise Creates Domestic Crisis

The eminent Rabbi Maurice L. Perlman, head of the British Section of the World Jewish Congress, stated to a Canadian audience as reported by The Toronto Evening Telegram of February 26, 1940, that: "The World Jewish Congress has been at war with Germany for seven years." Senator Wayne Morse of Oregon delivered an address on December 20, 1951, as reported in The National Jewish Post of Indianapolis of December 28, 1951, in which he stated: "One of the major causes for our going to war against Hitler was the persecution of the Jews in Germany." Dr. Donald C. Blaisdell, professor of government at the College of the City of New York, published an important document entitled American Policy for the near East in a publication called *Issues* published in New York, the official organ of the American Council for Judaism, in the fall issue in 1959, in which Dr. Blaisdell stated: "No minority of Irish, of German, of Polish, Italian, or Greek extraction has been able to manipulate policy to its advantage as have the Zionist leaders of American Jews. Nor does there appear to be any politically feasible means by which the American government can place the claims of its important clientele in proper perspective. Like American Jews who are presumed to be members of Israel's American clientele are never allowed to forget it, so the American government, Congress and Executive branch alike, is never permitted to free itself from the pressure, propaganda and power emanating from the same Zionist sources." This author has been in a position since 1912 to witness what was going on behind the scenes. This author served on the National Democratic Committee in the 1912 campaign that elected President Wilson to his first term. No doors have been closed to this author since then. This author was ushered into this world in 1890 by Dr. Simon Baruch, the father of Mr. Bemard M. Baruch. Mr. Bemard Baruch was a good friend of this author's family and would very often consult this author on this situation.

## Franklin Roosevelt Manipulated by Talmudic Jews

President Franklin D. Roosevelt was a captive of the Talmudists from the time he went to Albany as governor of the state of New York. President Roosevelt was long beholden to the Talmudists. The story of how President Roosevelt led the United States into the desperate predicament in which the United States today finds itself in the Middle East is not a long story. It is the story of how President Roosevelt railroaded the United States into the Second World War: Germany and Poland had agreed upon a formula giving Germany access across the Danzig Corridor. President Wilson, in 1919, created the Danzig Corridor which separated Germany into two halves. In order to keep Germany weak, at the instigation of Talmudists at the Versailles Peace Conference, President Wilson cut Germany into two halves, separated by a strip of German territory granted to Poland which divided Germany into two halves. Crossing the Danzig Corridor from western Germany to eastern Germany or vice versa was like traveling from one country to another. The inconveniences, the delays and the annoyances to Germany and Poland had finally worked out their acceptable arrangement that eliminated a majority of German objections to the Danzig Corridor. Germany and Poland reached a basis that would serve to prevent Germany's resort to more aggressive action. Adolf Hitler was the head of the German government at the time. Talmudists throughout the world opposed the peaceful adjustment between Germany and Poland of the Danzig Corridor situation. Unrestricted access of traffic between the western half and the eastern half of Germany would soon make Germany again the most powerful country in the world. Talmudists throughout the world dreaded the thought. In spite of the difficulties placed in the way of reaching a solution for the Danzig Corridor problem, Germany and Poland finally agreed upon a formula. Preparations were being made to consummate their understanding in a treaty. Both Germany and Poland were satisfied the formula agreed upon served both governments. Shortly before the agreement with Germany was to be signed, Poland secretly signed a treaty with Great Britain dated August 25, 1939. Great Britain agreed in that treaty to hasten the military assistance of Poland "with all the support and assistance in its power" if Poland were attacked by Germany. With that assurance from Great Britain, Poland broke off negotiations with Germany. Germany did not understand the reason for Poland's sudden change of mind and decided to proceed with the terms of the arrangement agreed upon with Poland. That was the start of World War II. Great Britain knowingly deceived

Poland when Great Britain actually promised military assistance to Poland if Poland were attacked by Germany. Great Britain could not come to Poland's assistance and Great Britain knew it when Great Britain's offer of military assistance to Poland was made. Poland fell into Great Britain's trap and discontinued negotiations with the Germans. Poland's unexplained discontinuance of negotiations with Germany to complete the Danzig Corridor agreement resulted in Germany's troops moving into the Danzig Corridor without an agreement with Poland. Great Britain knew exactly what would take place in that event, that it would mean the beginning or World War II. The rest is history. Talmudists of the world welcomed a war against Germany in 1939 to somehow crush the Nazi government as the Talmudists of the world crushed Germany in World War I in 1917 by railroading the United States into the war in Europe as Great Britain's ally. President Roosevelt tried his hardest in 1939 to railroad The United States into the war in Europe to accommodate Talmudists in the United States. Germany learned by experience in World War I that the entry of the United States into the war in Europe in 1939 could prove equally disastrous to Germany if the United States were railroaded into war in Europe as Great Britain's ally. Germany exercised extraordinary caution not to provide the United States with justification under international law to declare war against Germany. That situation presented President Roosevelt with a problem. President Roosevelt decided if it were impossible for him to get into the war in Europe through the front door that he would railroad the United States into the war in Europe through the back door. Through the back door meant through Japan. President Roosevelt finally did railroad the United States into the war in Europe through the back door, through Japan.

**Secretary of Defense Stimson During World War II Makes Startling Revelation**

Germany and Japan had a treaty under which if either Germany or Japan were attacked by a third power, the country which was not attacked by the third power automatically is at war with that third power. President Roosevelt planned to provoke Japan so Japan would attack the United States. Japan in December 1941 attacked Pearl Harbor. The United States immediately declared war against Japan and automatically was at war with Germany. The personal diary of the Hon. Mr. Henry L. Stimson and all his papers are in Yale University Library. Mr. Stimson each day entered in his personal diary in his own handwriting the important events in his life that day. Mr. Stimson was President Roosevelt's secretary of defense. Mr. Stimson's diary was introduced as evidence in the United States Senate investigation of the Pearl Harbor attack by Japan over the strong objections of friends of President Roosevelt. Mr. Stimson entered in his diary on November 25, 1941, two weeks before Japan's attack on Pearl Harbor, that at a meeting with President Roosevelt and his cabinet that morning at the White House, President Roosevelt told those present that he wished to be at war against Japan but that he "did not want it to appear that the United States fired the first shot."

## Zionist Conspirators Provoke Pearl Harbor Incident

President Roosevelt knowingly provoked Japan to attack the United States. President Roosevelt advised Japan they could purchase no more steel scrap or oil from the United States. Japan was in the midst of a war against China. Without scrap steel and without oil Japan would be unable to continue that war. Japan was totally dependent upon the United States for both steel scrap and oil. Professor Charles Callan Tansill, professor of diplomatic history at Georgetown University in Washington, wrote a classic work he called *Back Door to War*, published by Henry Regnery of Chicago in 1952. Professor Tansill spent five years after the war in the confidential files of the State Department doing research there on World War II. Professor Tansill's book has 652 pages all filled with alarming authenticated facts little known to the public during the war. In a scholarly detailed manner easily understood, Professor Tansill supplies facts which are incontrovertible proof showing how President Roosevelt railroaded the United States into World War II in Europe. President Roosevelt's desire to please Talmudists among his friends, influenced his better judgment. He overlooked that he was president of all the people of the United States. President Roosevelt realized if he expected political support by Talmudists in the United States to continue he must find some way to railroad the United States into the war then in progress in Europe against Germany. Surely nobody can any longer question that railroading the United States into World War II was President Roosevelt's contribution to the desperate predicament in which the United States today funds itself in the Middle East. President Harry S. Truman made his great contribution to the desperate predicament in which the United States today funds itself in the Middle East when he recognized as a sovereign state an armed uprising in Palestine by 800,000 armed aliens transplanted into Palestine in a conspiracy organized by Talmudists throughout the world. President Truman in 1946 suffered from a pathological obsession that he must be elected president of the United States in 1948 on his own account. Mr. Clarke M. Clifford, Secretary of War under President Lyndon B. Johnson, deserves a great deal of credit for the recognition of the State of Israel on May 14, 1948, by the United States. Mr. Eliahu Epstein, the United States representative of the Jewish Agency in Washington in 1948, told the story in his three-page article in the Jewish Chronicle of London in its 10th anniversary issue of June 1958 celebrating the 10th anniversary of the founding of the State of Israel. Mr. Clifford undoubtedly was anxious to help because President Truman had confided in his close friends that he wished to recognize the Zionist state in the "first hour of its birth" as he did. The State of Israel was officially "proclaimed" in Tel Aviv at midnight on May 14, 1948. President Truman recognized the birth of the State of Israel eleven minutes after midnight. President Truman finally advised this author that he did not wish to carry on the discussion of the Zionist question with him any further. He wrote to this author that he had turned over the entire Palestine question to "the Hon. David Niles." Talmudists were willing to carry out their part of their bargain with President Truman after he recognized the State of Israel. Although the odds in President Truman's election in 1948 were 20 to 1 against his election, President Truman romped home the winner over Governor Dewey assisted by the invisible and invincible Zionist political steam-roller that always elects their candidates. President Truman not only used the power and prestige of the United States to compel the United Nations to admit the State of Israel as a peace-loving nation, the regime of an armed uprising in Palestine by transplanted aliens, but he made billions of United States taxpayers dollars available to Talmudists to make the State of Israel powerful. When the day to vote for the admission of the State of Israel arrived they were short two votes. The plan was about to collapse. In the emergency, Mr. Charles H. Silver engaged Cardinal Spellman to make two trips to South America to change their votes in the United Nations against the admission of the State of Israel into the United Nation to vote in favor of the admission of the State of Israel into the United Nations as a member. The newspapers around the world on June 11, 1964, published Mr. Silver's "confession" of a "secret I have kept for fifteen years." The "secret" Cardinal Spellman kept with Mr. Silver was that Cardinal Spellman was sent to South America by Mr. Silver on behalf of the Talmudists in New York to "persuade" the South American countries to change their votes against admitting the State of Israel to the United Nations to vote in favor of admitting the State of Israel to the United Nations as a member. This author was a close personal friend of Cardinal Spellman for twenty-five years. Cardinal Spellman "confessed" to this author several years ago that he felt he had committed an irreparable sin by conspiring with the Talmudists in the United States to elect the State of Israel a member of the United Nations. In the midst of that bloody fighting in the Middle East in June 1967, Cardinal Spellman told this author when alone with him in his study that he felt personally responsible for all the lives lost in the 1967 invasion of the United Arab Republic and Syria by the State of Israel.

## H.J. 117 a Talmudic Creation-Eisenhower Steps in Line

The story of how President Dwight D. Eisenhower led the United States into the desperate predicament in which the United States today finds itself in the Middle East is not a complicated story. Talmudists in the United States pressured President Eisenhower into sponsoring Joint Resolution by Congress of H.J. Res. 117, on January

5, 1950, which was then refined by Congress to the Committee on Foreign Affairs. President Eisenhower knew less about what he was doing than a new born babe. It was pitiful for this author to witness a great general being figuratively pushed around by Talmudists unfit to shine his shoes. President Eisenhower was always friendly towards this author. This author met President Eisenhower when he was being considered by Mr. Thomas M. Watson, Sr., as a presidential candidate on the Democratic ticket. Mr. Watson was the founder of the International Business Machines Company. He told this author at that time that he believed General Eisenhower as a Civilian would make a great president. As president of the United States, General Eisenhower was faithful to these Talmudist supporters whose friendship he first cultivated in Europe during his political activities in Germany after the end of World War II. Talmudists curried his favor after World War II. They knew that as president of the United States, General Eisenhower in their hands would be like clay in the hands of the potter. In 1956 it appeared that Middle East countries were undergoing changes in their governments. The Zionist illegal occupation of Palestine still existed. Populations in Middle East countries were growing restless. Talmudists recognized something must be done to silence the unrest. President Eisenhower then obliged the Talmudists. Lebanon is the heart of Middle East political activity. To nip action in the bud, by native populations aiming to assert their independence from domination by Talmudists, Talmudists arranged with President Eisenhower to occupy Lebanon with fourteen thousand (14,000) troops and to station the Sixth Fleet off the coast. To make it legal, Talmudists had Congress pass a Joint resolution like the Tonkin Bay Resolution passed by Congress to legalize the war in Vietnam.

## President Eisenhower Performs Fulfillment of Zionist Demands in Middle East

President Eisenhower occupied Lebanon with fourteen thousand (14,000) United States troops and stationed the sixth Fleet off the Lebanon coast. President Eisenhower was warning the Middle East nations not to attempt to regain Palestine from the Zionists in illegal possession of Palestine. President Eisenhower must have had a consortium of the smartest Talmudists the state defense and justice departments prepare that joint resolution. The intent of that unclear language is to conceal the purpose of the joint resolution not to explain its purpose. The purpose was to have a joint resolution in record that would permit President Eisenhower to use the United States armed forces and navy to aid and abet the Zionist thieves to hold onto their stolen loot without any necessity to ask Congress to declare war. Every word President Eisenhower uttered to defend the crooks in occupation of Palestine was a lie which contributed to the desperate predicament in which the United States today finds itself in the Middle East. Talmudists in the United States were able to camouflage their illegal aggression in the Middle East behind the glamour of President Eisenhower's record as a great soldier. The story of how President John F. Kennedy led the United States into the desperate predicament in which the United States today finds itself in the Middle East is very distressing. President Kennedy's future was uncertain after digressing on August 25, 1960, from the straight and narrow path he had followed all his life. President Kennedy could not escape the consequences of his betrayal of the high principles to which he aimed to dedicate his life. President Kennedy surrendered to the lure of Talmudists who pledged to put him in the White House as the president of the United States. On August 23 1960, in the United States Senate office building in Washington President Kennedy, at that time a senator, gave this author a copy of the address he was to deliver in New York City on August 25, 1960. In the copy of that address he stated among other things: "Israel...three weeks ago I said in a public statement: Israel is here to stay...my flat prediction that Israel is here to stay...will endure and flourish...a special obligation on the Democratic Party...it was President Truman who first recognized the new State of Israel and gave it status in world affairs...may I and...my hope and my pledge to continue the democratic tradition...if the Democratic platform is to have any meaning...the White House must take the lead... American intervention... will not now be easy...I propose that we make it crystal clear...we will act promptly and decisively...I propose that we make it clear...our guarantee that we will act with whatever force and speed are necessary..the risk of war..." President (Senator) Kennedy was giving Talmudists his pledge that as the president of the United States he would send sons, husbands and brothers of the grass roots population of the United States to fight in Palestine under the flag of the United States in a war in Palestine to help crooks hold onto stolen loot, to aid and abet thieves retain possession of their stolen plunder. This author met President Kennedy for the first time in his father's office at 230 Park Avenue, in New York City, on the day after he was elected for the first time as a Congressman in November 1946. This author was in a conference with Ambassador Joseph Kennedy and Judge Landis, an associate of Ambassador Kennedy. In his private office they were consulting this author on the Middle East situation which had recently taken an ugly turn in the United Nations.

**President John Kennedy Pledges Zionists He Will Act in Their Favor Even at the Risk of War**

Ambassador Kennedy discussed the subject matter for a short while with those present. The Congressman then asked to leave as he was catching a train for Washington. This author invited the Congressman to lunch and he accepted. After lunch Congress Kennedy asked if this author had nothing else to do than ride to Washington with him on the train. This author was willing and rode to Washington with him. From that day in November 1946 to August 23, 1960, this author saw the Congressman, and the Senator, countless times in his office in Washington and New York City This author was happy to enlighten Senator Kennedy on the Palestine question. Without a doubt there were soon few people in the world who were better informed on this subject than Senator Kennedy. In the fourteen years this author had the honor of enjoying the confidence of President Kennedy he never failed to express his appreciation for this author's interest in his career. President Kennedy also appreciated the friendship this author demonstrated for his father, Ambassador Kennedy. Ambassador Kennedy was blackmailed by President Roosevelt. President Roosevelt told

Ambassador Kennedy not to write the book he planned to write. President Roosevelt removed Ambassador Kennedy as Ambassador to the Court of St. James in London for circulating what Neville Chamberlain told Ambassador Kennedy in London in 1938.

## The Senior Kennedy Liquidated Politically by Franklin Roosevelt for Reporting Talmudic Conspiracy

Ambassador Kennedy reported to Washington in 1938 that Neville Chamberlain told him that the United States and Talmudists throughout the world forced Great Britain into the Second World War. Chamberlain also told Ambassador Kennedy in 1938 that Great Britain had nothing with which to fight Germany, that Great Britain should not risk going to war against Germany. Chamberlain complained to Ambassador Kennedy that United States Ambassador to France William C. Bullit in 1938 was urging President Roosevelt that Germany must be "faced down" in their attitude towards Poland in the Danzig Corridor matter. President Roosevelt recalled Ambassador Kennedy to silence him. Ambassador Kennedy planned to return to the United States to write a book telling what he knew that he thought the grass roots population of the United States should be told. President Roosevelt sent for Ambassador Kennedy upon his return to the United States to come to Washington to see him. President Roosevelt told Ambassador Kennedy that he had heard that he was planning to write a book which he asked him not to do. After Ambassador Kennedy's unpleasant meeting with President Roosevelt in Washington after his recall from London for daring to circulate what Chamberlain had told him about Talmudists, his ambition in life was to see one of his sons in the White House as president of the United States. The story of how President Lyndon Baines Johnson led the United States into the desperate predicament in which the United States today finds itself in the Middle East is not a long story. It commences with a telephone call to this author in New York from Congressman Ed Gosset in Washington to come there at once. Congressman Gosset represented Amarillo, Texas, in the House of Representatives. Congressman Gosset was alarmed that the Senate Armed Services Committee the day before confirmed the appointment of Anna M. Rosenberg as Assistant Secretary of Defense without a public hearing. The only witness who appeared to testify concerning Anna Rosenberg's fitness to serve as Assistant Secretary of Defense was Ann Rosenberg herself. That by itself aroused suspicion among the country's leaders. Congress Gosset took this author to Senator Johnson's office and explained to him the reason for the visit. Senator Johnson was a member of the Senate Armed Services Committee which had confirmed Anna Rosenberg's appointment the previous day. Senator Johnson was very much interested in learning about Anna Rosenberg's associations with communists. Senator Johnson asked this author if he would assist him in looking into the matter further by producing a communist who knew Anna Rosenberg. Upon this author's return to New York that day, he mentioned Senator Johnson's request to his attorney, Mr. Hallam Richardson. Within a few hours, Mr. Richardson produced Mr. Ralph de Sola, a prominent communist, the head of film photography of documents by communist Organizations in the United States. After Anna Rosenberg's confirmation by the Senate Armed Services Committee was withdrawn, another hearing was held to confirm her second appointment. Anna Rosenberg testified she was born in Hungary and came to the United States in 1912 at the age of eleven years. The second hearing brought out some interesting facts — it confirmed her extended appointment for four years. In this author's meetings with Sen. Johnson, this author had occasion to discuss the Palestine question with him. Senator Johnson was very interested in the Palestine question. That subject was of great interest to the Senate Armed Services Committee. The occupation of Palestine by the Zionists concerned the Armed Services Committee.

**Lyndon Johnson Master-Minded Six Day War**
Senator Johnson was vice-president before the death of President Kennedy elevated him. He then became president of the United States. As president of the United States, Johnson was aware of the possibility of armed conflict in the Middle East in which the United States might become involved. President Johnson

understood the power Talmudists exerted in the United States and in the United Nations. One of his closest friends in Washington was Mr. Abe Fortas, a prominent Zionist, whom President Johnson appointed to the Supreme Court. President Johnson knew he was violating the letter and spirit of his oath of office as the president of all the people of the United States when he filled the pipe lines of the State of Israel with munitions of war paid for with the money of Christian taxpayers in the United States. President Johnson cannot plead ignorance of the facts. Though a very close mutual friend, this author kept President Johnson constantly informed on developments in the Middle East. President Johnson will be the first to admit he led the United States into the desperate predicament in which the United States today finds itself in the Middle East if he will glance at the promises, pledges and predictions he made to Talmudists in the United States while he occupied the White House as president of the United States. President Johnson now seeks to justify his generosity with United States taxpayers' money by referring to a "commitment." President Johnson knows that he is in error. The only commitment the taxpayers in the United States recognize is President Johnson's commitment to serve the best interests of the grass roots population of the United States. According to the Pentagon Papers he was not very successful in that respect. President Johnson does not display mature judgment when he squanders billions of the taxpayers' hard-earned dollars to aid and abet crooks to hold onto their stolen loot, their stolen plunder. President Johnson would feel differently if the Soviet Union financed an invasion of Texas by Mexicans who expelled Texans from their homes with only shirts on their backs to survive in refugee camps in the deserts of Arizona and New Mexico on six cents a day for food provided by the United Nations. Mexicans have a more legitimate claim to the territory called Texas today than the eastern European Talmudists ever had to Palestine. What would President Johnson's attitude have been if the Soviet Union contributed thirty-two billion dollars ($32,000,000,000) to go towards entrenching these Mexican invaders in Texas, and then supplying the Mexican invaders with sophisticated military hardware to threaten the other forty-nine United States if they interfered with the illegal possession of Texas by the Mexican invaders in illegal occupation of Texas, without having paid one cent to the lawful landowners for a square foot of Texas. The story how President Nixon led the United States into the desperate predicament in which the United States today finds itself is of great interest to the grass roots population of the United States every time President Nixon grants the Zionists, in illegal occupation of Palestine, another five hundred million dollars ($500,000,000) of United States taxpayers' money. Is President Nixon serving two masters? President Nixon is as guilty as the other six masters of deception who led the United States into the desperate predicament in which the United States today finds itself in the Middle East. President Nixon is both an eminent lawyer and President of the United States. President Nixon cannot produce any evidence of a legitimate "commitment" to anyone to support President Nixon's generous use of United States taxpayers' money for financing the permanent possession by thieves of their stolen loot. Does President Nixon mean the "commitment" by political leaders to the Talmudists in the United States who control the media for mass information? President Nixon belittles himself as well as the United States Administration for whom he speaks when he talks about a "commitment" of the United States to underwrite the perpetual possession of the illegal and immoral theft of Palestine by Talmudists. President Nixon's generosity has reached epidemic proportions. Each of the additional five hundred million dollars ($500,000,000) of United States taxpayers' money he donates to the so-called State of Israel is that many more nails in the coffin of the United States. These seven masters of deception mock the elementary and equitable principles upon which the United States was founded when they throw hard-earned United States taxpayers' dollars by the billions to criminals in possession of their stolen loot as if it were stage money. Have they no shame or conscience? When there were civil wars recently in the Congo, in Nagana, in Pakistan and other countries in this century, did the United States "recognize" the populations as independent indigenous populations who planned to secede and form their sovereign independent states? Then why recognize transplanted alien invaders financed by Talmudists? If these seven masters of deception reflected the honorable attitude the United States should exhibit, they would not traffic with thieves, murderers, and scoundrels as they are doing with the hooligans from the State of Israel. The United States refused to "recognize" the independence of Katanga, of Biafra, of East Pakistan, of Quebec and of total Ireland, but they rushed to "recognize" the hooligans of an armed Palestine uprising by transplanted aliens as a legitimate sovereign state. What next?

## Talmudic Hidden Hand Controls the U.S. Vote in the United Nations

The one hundred and twenty-five other members of the United Nations know that the United States was as crooked as a cork screw to recognize the so-called State of Israel as a lawful representative government of the indigenous population. The other nations of the world all know by this time that Talmudists elect the presidents of the United States and members of Congress. If these Talmudists in the United States were paupers, they could not elect a dog catcher in the United States. How rotten can the political system in the United States get before it drops into the lap of a more honorable nation like a rotten piece of fruit falls from a tree?

### Rothschild Conspiracy Fulfilled

The so-called State of Israel is positive that the United States must at the request of the State of Israel veto any resolution introduced in the Security Council to expel the so-called State of Israel. Consequently, this so-called State of Israel feels as smug as a bug in a rug regardless of what they do. The Talmudists control the delegation in the United States. Nobody but a fool or an ignoramus doubts that today. The Talmudists always instruct the delegates of the United States how to vote in the Security Council. If a resolution is ever introduced to expel the so-called State of Israel, the United States must veto the resolution. The grass roots population of the United States deserves to know the truth about the Middle East crisis. They will pay with their lives unless they soon acquire a better understanding about why the Middle East crisis exists. The United

States finds it convenient to blame everything that goes wrong anywhere in the world on Communism. Communism provides a convenient whipping boy for politicians. The arch villains behind the world's difficulties are the Rothschilds. For the moment, this author will only deal with the Rothschild's interest in the subject matter of this article, the Middle East desperate predicament of the world. This author can speak with confidence on this subject as his knowledge was obtained first hand from members of the Rothschild dynasty in London, New York and elsewhere. The extent of the Rothschild wealth cannot be estimated with any degree of certainty. A conservative guess of the total value of the Rothschild fortunes would be billions of dollars, if that amount can be imagined. The important thing is the major portion of this wealth is in the Far East. The Rothschild interest in Europe, and the Western Hemisphere, are tremendous. However, in comparison to their wealth in the Far East, it is significant. A most vital single thing in the world to the Rothschild dynasty is access to the Far East. Access to the Far East through the Mediterranean is known as Great Britain's lifeline. The Rothschild dynasty had plunged Great Britain into many wars only to preserve their lifeline to the Far East. History tells that story. The Suez Canal was not constructed by the Rothschilds. They did their utmost to prevent its construction. The Suez Canal was constructed by the Frenchman, de Lesseps, and the Khedive of Egypt. The Rothschilds refused to invest one cent of their money in the company which obtained the concession to construct the Suez Canal. The Suez Canal was completed in 1869. It, from the very start, proved a great success. The Rothschilds swindled a forty percent (40%) interest in the Suez Canal Company from the Khedive of Egypt. They found a forty percent (40%) interest insufficient for their purpose as the value of the Suez Canal had been demonstrated after it was in use two years. The Rothschilds decided they must control their lifeline to their fortune in the Far East. Without justification or provocation of any description, the Rothschilds had Great Britain occupy Egypt exactly as a defeated power is occupied by the victor. The British ran the schools, the banks, the railroads, the courts, and Egypt ceased to be Egypt except in name. Naturally, the Suez

Canal came under complete control of Great Britain. The original concession for the Suez Canal was for ninety-nine years. The more important the Suez Canal became to the Rothschilds, the more the Rothschilds worried what was going to happen when the ninety-nine year concession for the Suez Canal expired in 1969 and reverted to Egypt as the concession provided. Great Britain spent large fortunes and spilled much blood in many wars to maintain uninterrupted and undisturbed possession of the Suez Canal. The Rothschilds knew that Egypt would be free to grant a new concession for the Suez Canal to a power unfriendly to Great Britain, like France, Germany or Russia, when the concession expired. The Rothschilds feared the consequences should the Suez Canal fall into the hands of an unfriendly power and Great Britain had many powers in mind who could make good use of the Suez Canal politically also against the British Empire.

## Rothschild Fortune Risked Collapse Without Middle East Controls Under Zionist Supervision

The Rothschild dynasty's fortune and Great Britain's authority would diminish in the Far East if Great Britain no longer controlled the Suez Canal. Looking ahead, the Rothschilds planned their future without the Suez Canal. The First World War ended in 1918 and the Rothschilds had their plan ready. Their plan was very simple. Under the October 1916 London Agreement, Great Britain planned to turn over Palestine to the Zionists after the war. The eastern European Talmudists had no money. Without money Palestine was a headache to the Zionists. The Rothschilds in London promised the Zionists unlimited financial assistance with which to develop Palestine, but on one condition — that as soon as Palestine was turned over to the Zionists, they apply for admission to the British Empire as a member. The Rothschilds planned to construct a canal in Palestine from Ashkelon on the Mediterranean to Aqaba on the Gulf of Aqaba. They planned to construct a modern steel and concrete canal with two lanes for ships. The canal would be on British territory in perpetuity enjoying the advantages of defense by Great Britain if needed and international recognition as a member of the British

Empire. Great Britain occupied Palestine from 1921 to 1948 as the Mandatory of the League of Nations. During that period the British Empire fell apart. By the time the Zionists established a Zionist state in Palestine, the British Empire had fallen apart and no longer existed. Palestine under the Zionists could not apply for admission to the British Empire. There was no British Empire. When the Rothschilds realized what was happening, they were compelled to alter their plans. The Rothschilds were determined that Great Britain must turn over Palestine to the Zionists for a sovereign Zionist state. The idea of a United Nations was then a reality and the Rothschilds planned upon getting the sovereign Zionist state admitted to the United Nations. The United Nations would provide Palestine with the same advantages that the British Empire would have provided once upon a time. If the sovereign Zionist state could be admitted to the United Nations, Palestine's future was assured. Rothschilds did not know what to do. Then in October 1916, the World Zionist Organization entered the picture. When Great Britain was considering surrender to Germany, the World Zionist Organization and the British War Cabinet entered into the October 1916 London Agreement. The Rothschild dynasty was astonished when, on April 6, 1917, the United States declared war against Germany. By July 1917 it appeared that Germany would be defeated after the entry of the United States into the war. The Rothschild dynasty sought out Mr. Chaim Weizmann and cultivated his friendship. The Rothschilds realized that the World Zionist Organization must be recognized. The Rothschilds purchased a Prince Albert frock coat and a silk hat for Chaim Weizmann and treated him as though he was already the head of the government of Palestine, which he eventually became. The Rothschilds renewed their interest in the plan to finance the Zionist movement in Palestine in exchange for the concession to construct their modern canal across Palestine in competition with the Suez Canal. Great Britain was certain to defeat Germany. Great Britain had agreed to turn over Palestine to the Talmudists of the world for railroading the United States into the war in Europe as Great Britain's ally. The only link missing now was the existence in Palestine of an independent sovereign Zionist state. The Rothschilds financed transplanting 600,000 eastern European Talmudists into Palestine and arranged to remove the last of General Allenby's 200,000 British troops from Palestine.

In collaboration with President Truman in the United States the armed 600,000 transplanted alien Talmudists on May 18, 1948, began their expulsion from Palestine of the Christian and Moslem disarmed and defenseless 1,350,000 population and at the same time declared their armed uprising the State of Israel. The Rothschilds were now satisfied. The only unfinished business was to force the Middle East nations to recognize the State of Israel. The Rothschilds commenced their final stage by building the present oil pipeline from Ashkelon on the Mediterranean to Aqaba, along the route of their future modern long-planned steel and concrete two-lane canal. The Middle East situation is the result of the Rothschild efforts to secure permanent and secure access to the Far East. This nonsense about the "repatriation" of "Gods chosen people" to "their promised land" has been revealed the greatest hoax ever perpetrated on mankind. The single purpose of the Rothschilds was to secure permanent and secure access to their vast natural resources in the Far East. This author has had the patience and the time to inform seven presidents of the United States about the underlying reason for the Middle East aggression by the Talmudist throughout the world. These seven masters of deception were all briefed by this author on the reason for the aggression in Palestine. This author spent a small fortune acquainting members of Congress and political and industrial leaders in the United States with all these facts, supplying them with photostat reproductions of documentary evidence to support every statement made by this author. It cries out to heaven that this country and the world has been put to the expense of billions of billions of dollars to see the Rothschilds have secure and permanent access to their unlimited wealth in the Far East. If the Talmudists of the world say they are willing to see another world war fought to establish "God's chosen people" in "their promised land" to rule the world from Palestine, then it is time to tell the grass roots of the United States population what all the excitement is about. This issue must be dragged into the light for the grass roots of the population of the United States to see why they are expected to die in an unnecessary war with a smile on their face.

www.ingramcontent.com/pod-product-compliance
Lightning Source LLC
LaVergne TN
LVHW051249080426
835513LV00016B/1827